BRISTOL AT WAR

BRISTOL AT WAR

OHN PENNY

First published in Great Britain in 2002 by The Breedon Books Publishing Company Limited Breedon House, 3 The Parker Centre, Derby, DE21 4SZ.

Paperback edition published in Great Britain in 2010 by The Derby Books Publishing Company Limited, 3 The Parker Centre, Derby, DE21 4SZ.

ISBN 978-1-85983-872-3

Printed and bound by OZGraf, Poland.

CONTENTS

ACKNOWLEDGEMENTS   7

WORLD WAR TWO TIME CHART   8

GLOSSARY AND ABBREVIATIONS   9

Chapter 1   WAR ON THE HORIZON – *The Home Front Prepares – 1935 to 1939.*   11

Chapter 2   DEFENCES INSTALLED AND OPERATIONAL – *June 1938 to July 1940.*   33

Chapter 3   THE EAGLE TIGHTENS ITS GRIP – *August to October 1940.*   56

Chapter 4   THE ONSLAUGHT BEGINS – *November 1940.*   69

Chapter 5   A BLEAK CHRISTMAS – *December 1940.*   94

Chapter 6   A MISERABLE NEW YEAR – *January and February 1941.*   109

Chapter 7   THE END OF THE STORM – *March and April 1941.*   127

Chapter 8   THE DIMINISHING THREAT – *May 1941 to December 1942.*   152

Chapter 9   ONWARDS TO VICTORY – *January 1943 to May 1945.*   172

INDEX   190

DEDICATED *to Jim Facey*

Bristol Evening Post's chief photographer
who took so many unforgettable pictures of
bombed Bristol and without whose
dedication and professionalism under
difficult conditions future generations would
be deprived of images of the most horrific
chapter in the city's history.

ACKNOWLEDGEMENTS

Without help freely given by a number of individuals and institutions during the last 30 years it would have been impossible to produce this book. My special thanks go to the late George Morley, of the South West Aircraft Recovery Group, for his unstinting support in the early days; to Ian James who shared with me all his research into Bristol's air defences; and especially to Ken Wakefield who has allowed me to use so much of the Luftwaffe material he has collected over the years. Simon Parry of Air Research Publications also provided me with unique material concerning the events of 1944, while Mr F.C. Hooper generously lent me many important items from his collection of local fire brigade material. Likewise, the staff of the Bristol Central Library, the Bristol Record Office, the Royal Air Force Museum at Hendon, the Imperial War Museum at Lambeth, the Public Record Office at Kew and the Militärarchiv at Freiburg, in Southern Germany, have regularly gone out of their way to be helpful to me during the course of numerous visits. Last, but by no means least, my thanks go to Dave Facey for permission to use the wonderful photographs taken by his father, who during World War Two was the *Bristol Evening Post's* chief photographer.

WORLD WAR TWO TIME CHART

1938

14 February	Germany annexes Austria.
29 September	Munich Agreement signed by Germany, Italy, Britain and France.

1939

16 March	Bohemia and Moravia annexed by Germany.
25 May	Anglo-Polish Treaty signed in London.
1 September	Germany invades Poland. Great Britain and France mobilise.

1940

9 April	Germany invades Denmark and Norway.
10 May	Germany invades Holland, Belgium and Luxembourg.
14 May	Holland ceases fighting.
27 May	Evacuation of British and French troops from Dunkirk begins.
28 May	Belgium ceases fighting.
10 June	Italy declares war on Britain and France.
25 June	France ceases fighting.
1 July	Germans invade the Channel Islands.

1941

6 April	Germany invades Greece and Yugoslavia.
22 June	Germany invades the Soviet Union.
7 December	Japan declares war on Britain and the United States of America.
23 December	Hong Kong surrenders.

1942

16 January	Iraq declares war on the Axis powers.
15 February	Singapore surrenders.
6 September	German advance halted at Stalingrad.
8 November	Allies land in French North Africa.
16 November	US naval forces secure a great victory over the Japanese at Guadalcanal.

1943

13 May	Axis resistance ceases in Tunisia.
10 July	Allies invade Sicily.
3 September	Allies invade Italian mainland.
8 September	Italy surrenders.

1944

6 June	D-Day. Allies land in Normandy.
15 August	Allies invade Southern France.
21 August	Rumania surrenders.
4 September	Allied troops enter Brussels.
6 September	Bulgaria requests an armistice.
11 August	Luxembourg City liberated.
14 October	Athens liberated.
15 October	Hungary requests an armistice.
20 October	Belgrade liberated.

1945

17 January	Russians enter Warsaw.
10 April	Russians enter Vienna.
2 May	Russians enter Berlin.
8 May	VE Day. War in Europe officially ends.
8 August	Russia declares war on Japan.
15 August	VJ Day. War against Japan officially ends.

GLOSSARY AND ABBREVIATIONS

A.A.	Anti-Aircraft.
A.F.S.	Auxiliary Fire Service.
A.R.P.	Air Raid Precautions.
A.T.S.	Auxiliary Territorial Service.
Aufkl.Gr.Ob.d.L.	Aufklärungsgruppe Oberbefehlshaber der Luftwaffe (Reconnaissance Wing of the Commander in Chief of the Luftwaffe).
B.A.C.	Bristol Aeroplane Company.
B.B.C.	British Broadcasting Corporation.
B.D.S.T.	British Double Summer Time.
B.E.M.	British Empire Medal.
Bf	Bayerische Flugzeugwerke. The early name for the Messerschmitt company.
B.S.T.	British Summer Time.
B1 El	Brandbomb 1kg Elektron (1kg magnesium incendiary bomb).
D-Day	The day upon which the Allied invasion of Europe was to begin.
Dead Reckoning	Navigation by calculating the track and ground speed actually achieved since 'last known position'.
Do	Dornier. A German aircraft manufacturer.
Epr.Gr.	Erprobungs Gruppe. (Experimental & Development Wing)
Ergr.u.Lehr Kdo	Erprobungs und Lehr Kommando (Experimental and Training unit). Approximately nine aircraft.
Fighter Night	Night patrol by single-engined fighters over a threatened city.
Flak	Anti-Aircraft artillery.
G.C.I.	Ground Controlled Interception (Radar).
Geschwader	Group of about 100 operational aircraft. Normally comprised three operational Gruppen, a Staff Flight, plus a fourth training Gruppe.
G.M.T.	Greenwich Mean Time.
Gruppe	Wing of 30 aircraft. Normally comprised three Staffeln and a Staff Flight. Abbreviated in roman numerals ie II/KG 27.
Gruppenkommandeur	Officer commanding a Gruppe.
H.A.A.	Heavy Anti-Aircraft.
H.E.	High Explosive.
He	Heinkel. A German aircraft manufacturer.
H.M.	His Majesty's.
H.Q.	Headquarters.
Illuminator	An aircraft dropping target marking flares without using electronic equipment.
Interception Patrol	Night patrol by Hampden aircraft over a threatened city.
Ju	Junkers. A German aircraft manufacturer.
KG	Kampfgeschwader (Bomber Group). Approximately 90 aircraft.
KGr	Kampfgruppe (Bomber Wing). A specialised independent unit. Approximately 30 aircraft.
Knickebein	A VHF electronic bombing and navigation aid employing two beams.
Kü Fl Gr	Küsten Flieger Gruppe (Coastal Attack Wing). Approximately 30 aircraft.
L.A.A.	Light Anti-Aircraft.

Land Mine   A parachute sea mine fitted with an impact fuse and used against a land target.

L.D.V.   Local Defence Volunteers.

LG   Lehrgeschwader (Training Group). Approximately 90 aircraft. A formation manned by pre-war training personnel. It became a normal bomber unit on the outbreak of war.

Luftwaffe   German Air Force.

(M)   Mixed (anti-aircraft unit).

M.B.E.   Member of the British Empire.

Me   Messerschmitt. A German aircraft manufacturer.

mm   millimetres.

m.p.h.   miles per hour.

No.   Number.

N.C.O.   Non-Commissioned Officer.

N.F.S.   National Fire Service.

O.B.E.   Order of the British Empire.

Oil Bomb   a large incendiary weapon filled with oil which ignited on impact.

Operation Layers   Original name for Fighter Night.

PC   Panzerbombe-Cylindrisch (Armour Piercing bomb).

R.A.F.   Royal Air Force.

R.A.S.C.   Royal Army Service Corps.

R.E.   Royal Engineers.

SC   Sprengbombe-Cylindrische (General Purpose bomb).

SD   Sprengbombe-Dickwandig (Semi-Armour Piercing bomb).

S.I.P   Self Igniting Phosphorous (grenade).

(SM)   Smoke.

S.S.   The RAF's Special Service Flight.

Stab   Staff Flight, normally three aircraft.

Staffel   Squadron of 9 aircraft. The Luftwaffe's smallest operational unit, with three to each Gruppe. Abbreviated in Arabic numerals ie 9/KG 55.

Staffelkapitän   Officer commanding a Staffel.

Starfish   A decoy fire lit to mislead enemy bomber crews.

Unternehmen Seelölow   Operation Sealion. The planned German invasion of Britain.

Unternehmen Steinbock   Operation Ibex. The code name given to the German raids on Britain carried out during 1944.

U.S.   United States.

U.S.A.A.F.   United States Army Air Force.

V.H.F.   Very High Frequency.

W.A.A.F.   Woman's' Auxiliary Air Force.

W.V.S.   Woman's Voluntary Service.

X Beam   An electronic beam associated with X-Verfahren.

X-Verfahren   X-System. A VHF electronic bombing aid employing a main and three crossed beams.

Y Beam   The electronic beam associated with Y-Verfahren.

Y-Verfahren   Y-System. An advanced VHF electronic bombing aid employing a single beam.

Y.W.C.A.   Young Woman's' Christian Association.

Z   Z Battery (anti-aircraft rockets).

ZG   Zerstörergeschwader (Long-Range Fighter Group). Approximately 90 aircraft.

CHAPTER 1

WAR ON THE HORIZON

The Home Front Prepares — 1935 to 1939

The traumatic four-year period between June 1940 and May 1944 saw Bristol face an ordeal by fire at the hands of one of the world's most awesome fighting machines, Hitler's Luftwaffe. This was a testing time for all its citizens, as well as for those drafted in to assist with the defences, and shortly after the worst of the bombing had ended Alderman T.H.J. Underdown, the Lord Mayor, resolved that:

'The City Council desire to record their admiration and appreciation of the efficient services rendered by the officers and whole-time and part-time personnel of the Air Raid Precautions and Auxiliary Fire Service, members of the voluntary and religious organisations, officers and men of H.M. Forces, staffs of the various hospitals, staffs and employees of the utility undertakings, the personnel loaned to the city by other authorities, officers and employees of the Corporation, and many other voluntary helpers during the recent air raids. The efficient organisation and splendid services rendered undoubtedly saved the city from much greater destruction and distress, and the Council feel they cannot express too highly their grateful thanks and that of the citizens generally for the devotion to duty and the courage displayed by all concerned.'

All this was said some 70 years ago, yet it is only today, with full access to official British and German records, that it is at last possible to look objectively at the facts and to discover the way in which the forces of a ruthless dictatorship attempted to destroy Bristol's commercial and industrial base, and just how its citizens and defenders organised and conducted themselves in the face of such brutal and naked aggression.

Founded over 1,000 years before, by the 1930s Bristol had become firmly established as the most

His Majesty King George IV being greeted by Alderman T.H.J. Underdown, the Lord Mayor of Bristol, on 16 December 1940. *(BUP)*

The plaques mounted on the wall of St Peter's Church in Castle Park commemorate those who were evacuated from Bristol during 1941 and the civilians and military personnel who lost their lives locally as a result of enemy action between 1940 and 1944. *(Author's Collection)*

important administrative centre in south-west England, as well as home to huge harbour complex and the largest concentration of aircraft manufacturing plants in the country. It was the seventh-largest conurbation in England, with only London, Birmingham, Liverpool, Manchester, Sheffield and Leeds containing larger populations. National Registration statistics compiled in 1939 established that some 415,500 people resided within the boundaries of the City & County of Bristol, while another 33,000 or so lived in the adjoining parts of Gloucestershire and Somerset. Of these, the vast majority were concentrated to the north of the city in the populous districts of Filton, Mangotsfield, Kingswood and Hanham, with only a few thousand being located to the south at Whitchurch and Bishopsworth, both of which were then little more than adjacent villages.

Being a place of such strategic importance, in any future conflict Bristol would undoubtedly be a prime target, and as by the middle of the 1930s many influential politicians and high-ranking military officers had become convinced that the slow fighter aircraft then in service would be incapable of preventing attacking bombers from reaching their targets, widespread damage was to be expected if bombing ever took place. The anxiety felt during this period was probably never better expressed than by Stanley Baldwin, three times Prime Minister, but at that time Lord President of the Council, who during a House of Commons debate in 1932 stated that it should be understood by the man in the street that: 'There is no power on earth that can prevent him from being bombed. Whatever people tell him, the bomber will always get through.'

The belief that any future war would be mainly a bomber contest, with fighters playing only a subsidiary rôle, had far reaching consequences for British defensive policy and resulted in the RAF expansion plan of 1935 calling for more bomber than fighter squadrons to be based in mainland Britain. Nevertheless, following the formation of Fighter Command in July 1936, a change began to take place in the way in which the defences were organised, and with the entry into service two years later of fast new eight-gun fighters and a revolutionary radio location (radar) early warning system in the offing, by late 1939 the situation had become reversed.

HURRICANE I (MERLIN)
Single-Seat Fighter
Span 40'-0"   Length 31'-5"   Height 11'-3"

Silhouette of the Hawker Hurricane. *(Author's Collection)*

Concerns over the possibility of war intensified in March 1935 when Germany's new air force, the Luftwaffe, was publicly revealed, and in that year the Air Raid Precautions Department, the forerunner of the wartime Ministry of Home Security, was established by the National Government as part of the Home Office. This new organisation was soon at work and on 9 July 1935 it issued a circular to all local authorities detailing the precautionary measures that would have to be taken to safeguard their areas in the event of air attack and as a consequence on 10 December an ARP Committee was established in Bristol. To begin with there was much haggling between local authorities and the central government over what proportion of the cost of introducing local ARP measures should be borne by Central Government, but shortly after the passing of the ARP Act in December 1937 which compelled local authorities to undertake ARP planning, the Treasury agreed to bear at least 65 per cent of the cost of such work. The Act required a complex system of organisations to be set up and co-ordinated in each local authority area, relying on wardens to control the reporting of incidents and the safety of the population, rescue teams to extricate casualties from collapsed buildings and decontamination squads to deal with the horrific possibility of attacks with poison gas. First aid and ambulance services, the police, and the all important fire brigades were also to be reinforced.

All Take Shelter

The Munich crisis brought with it for the first time the realisation that war was a distinct possibility, and this had the effect of at last galvanising Bristolians into action. As a result, trenches were dug in College Green and in municipal parks and open spaces, so that by the end of September 1938 trench shelter accommodation in such places had been provided for some 40,000 citizens, albeit at a cost of £50,000 to the City Council. This, however, fell short of the provision laid down by the Home Office so, to reach this level, non-domestic shelters of a variety of types were introduced. In addition to the trench shelters, these included public and communal surface and cellar shelters, as well as a variety of shelters built to house the city's school children and hostel dwellers. The basements of

This public brick built air raid shelter can
still be seen in Page Park, Staple Hill.
(Author's Collection)

buildings, church crypts, tunnels and even
caves were also used, some unofficially, and
it was these unconventional, shelters which
were soon to provide the authorities with a
number of special problems.

   To provide individual families with some sort of protection from bomb blast and flying debris the
Government went on to make available three types of domestic air raid shelter, the most robust of
which was the surface shelter constructed from brick and provided with a reinforced concrete roof,
examples of which can still be seen in gardens in and around Bristol. The second type, which became
available in November 1938, was the Anderson shelter, named after Sir John Anderson the Minister
for Civilian Defence, and during the war about 41,450 of these were issued to households in the city.
Assembled from curved corrugated steel sheets and measuring 6ft high, 4.5ft wide, and 6.5ft long,
these shelters were designed to be buried in the ground to a depth of at least 3ft and covered with
1.5ft of soil and turf, a process which rendered them liable to flooding during the winter months,
and therefore a most uncomfortable place for up to six people to spend a night huddled together.
The final type of shelter to be introduced was the Morrison, which took its name from Herbert
Morrison who was appointed Minister of Home Security in October 1940. It was designed for

Many private brick built air raid shelters still exist in Bristol. This example is in a lane behind Dominion
Road, Fishponds. *(Author's Collection)*

Although this house was destroyed during the Filton attack on 25 September 1940, Mrs Clark and her baby escaped unhurt from their Anderson shelter. *(Jim Facey)*

indoor use by those families who had neither a garden in which to erect an Anderson, or a cellar that could be reinforced. However, as the Morrison shelters resembled a large steel table fitted with mesh sides within which could be accommodated up to four people, they had the disadvantage of taking up a great deal of floor space and even caused some users to become decidedly claustrophobic!

Wardens Fall In

1938 also saw the start of the recruitment of personnel for the Wardens Service, the backbone of civil defence which, in Bristol, was under the direction of the Chief Constable. It was based around ARP Divisions with a divisional warden in charge of each, these being further sub-divided into groups, each headed by a group warden, and sectors, with approximately 500 people in each. Progress in Bristol, however, was slow and by September 1938 of the 2,191 men who had volunteered and been accepted only 1,064 were trained and 460 actually allocated to their respective sectors. Nevertheless, although still under strength, on 3 September 1939, when war eventually broke out, all 187 warden's posts were fully manned, each of these serving three or more sectors from such places as church halls and schools. At a later stage specially

constructed posts of steel and brick were built, six divisional headquarters were established and whole-time wardens, both men and women, were engaged, raising the actual strength by the end of the war to 3,756 men and 1,582 women. The bulk of the Wardens were unpaid volunteers and as the majority of these, unless in reserved occupations, were over 40 years of age, many already possessed useful military experience, having served in World War One. By contrast full-time wardens were relatively few, normally restricted to no more than two per post.

The Wardens' Service was designed to help the general public with advice, to give them information and, under raiding conditions, to give them warning of danger, to render assistance to those who might be injured or rendered homeless, to report air raid damage and to allay panic. In addition, a large number of Wardens volunteered for and trained as Bomb Reconnaissance Officers, a dangerous job which entailed the inspection of incidents where unexploded high-explosive bombs were suspected, while a special observation post on the tower of the Royal Fort, set up to detect and report the first fall of flares and bombs for Fighter Command, was also maintained and manned by Wardens. Nevertheless, in spite of all their varied duties and the amount of voluntary service given, members still found time to collect a large sum of money for the purpose of purchasing two Spitfire aircraft, R7194, *Bristol Civil Defence* and R7260, *Bristol Air Raid Warden* both first flown in March 1941.

Women in Great Demand

In November 1938 a Schedule of Reserved Occupations was published, this being designed to check the over enthusiastic volunteering for military service by skilled workers who were essential to the smooth running of the country, the vital services they provided ranging from farming and engineering to medicine and civil administration. Although the Military Training Act of May 1939 required young men to undertake six months' compulsory military training, as this limited form of

conscription applied only to those aged 20 and 21, on 3 September Parliament passed the National Service (Armed Forces) Act, which extended it all men between the ages of 18 and 41. Nevertheless, in spite of this swift action it was to be June 1941 before the oldest men had even been registered. Likewise, not all of those fit to serve were accepted for the armed forces, as employers could request the 'deferment' of the call-up of individual key workers in any of the Scheduled occupations. In addition, provision was also made for conscientious objection to military service on both pacifist and political grounds, the claims of these groups being heard by local tribunals. The war also brought about the relaxation of the Factories Act of 1937, and as a result working hours were extended so that increasing numbers of operatives, many of them women, were soon engaged in strenuous work on shifts often lasting for up to eleven hours. This is well illustrated by the aircraft industry, where some 40 per cent of the workers were female, while 52 per cent of those engaged in the manufacture of chemicals and explosives, and 33 per cent of those in ship building and heavy engineering, were also women.

In another attempt to involve women with war work, in 1938 the Home Office had asked the redoubtable Stella, Marchioness of Reading, to start an organisation which would might attract females into the ARP services, and thus was born the Woman's Voluntary Service for Air Raid Precautions, the contribution of which during the subsequent war was truly prodigious. Blood Transfusion campaigns, the salvage of paper and other scarce materials, the relief of evacuees and canteen services were but a few of the tasks undertaken by the WVS. It also recruited and trained drivers for ambulances, assisted in the movement of patients from hospitals and collected an enormous amount of clothes which it repaired and distributed to air raid victims, while always being on hand with a never ending supply of tea. These are but a few examples of the work of this remarkable organisation, and in view of what its members went on to do throughout the war it is difficult to understand how in previous national crises the country managed to survive without the WVS!

As a large amount of labour was also required on the land, in 1939 the Women's Land Army was re-introduced, its main task being to replace male farm workers who had joined the armed forces. Although few women, especially those from the cities, had any experience of the work they might be expected to carry out, the first woman to register with the Land Army was Valerie Hodge, an artist living in Bristol. She, in fact, joined as soon as National Service booklets were issued in the spring of 1939, and was later presented to King George VI at a National Service rally held in Hyde Park.

In spite of the fact that the Bristol area contained many important facilities and installations that were subsequently to prove of considerable interest to the Germans, at the end of 1938 when the Government had listed twelve industrial centres from which unessential people should be evacuated at the outbreak of war, the city was not included. Instead, as it was then out of the range of bombers based in Germany, it was classified as a 'neutral' area, which in practice meant that although no evacuation was to be carried out, neither were evacuees to be brought in from other parts of the country. With the majority of the population remaining in place, should any air attacks take place it was to be the responsibility of various civil organisations to mitigate the worst effects of the bombing by forestalling demoralisation, countering disorder and panic, limiting damage and helping people to survive. In addition to the Air Raid Precautions service, or the Civil Defence General Service as it was officially re-named on 2 September 1941, the other bodies charged with this task were the local fire brigade and police force.

Expanding the Police and Fire Services

Nationwide the existing fire services were to be augmented by a largely volunteer Auxiliary Fire Service, but unfortunately although the AFS was to be trained by the local peacetime fire brigade and under its authority. It was partly equipped and regulated on a national basis by the Home Office. It therefore had two masters and being born in dispute, to some extent remained so throughout its

existence. In Bristol, AFS recruiting got off to a poor start, but by the start of the war the 85 whole-time officers and men of the city's police operated Fire Brigade had been boosted by the 4,215 full and part-time men and women then enrolled in the AFS. The organisation was also quite well equipped and by the time the night Blitz began in November 1940 there were 26 Auxiliary Fire Stations in Bristol, each provided with a heavy pump on a trailer, while also available to the AFS were five fire floats, ten self propelled heavy pumps, 54 large trailer units and 140 light trailer units.

Providing emergency water supplies in Bristol was one of the many important jobs the fire service undertook during the war, and this entailed surveying all possible sources, such as rivers, streams, ponds, lakes, culverts and even swimming pools, as well as making

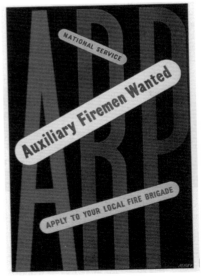

Concrete dams, part of Bristol's emergency water supply. *(NFS)*

provision for specially constructed holding tanks ranging in size from 1,000 gallon units mounted on lorries to 250,000 gallon basins constructed by the Corporation. In addition, to help in overcoming the fracture of the water mains by high explosive bombs the Home Office devised a system of 6in diameter steel pipelines to cover the major risk areas and by the end of 1944, due to the diligence of the local firemen, some 46 pipelines totalling over 24 miles had been laid around the city and in the Avonmouth Docks area.

By April 1939, it had been realised that Bristol's Police Service, then some 670 strong, would not be able to carry out single-handed all the duties which would fall upon it under war time conditions, so it was decided to augment them by enrolling an equal number of men, who as Police War Reserves, could be called upon to perform the duties of constables. Women were also recruited for the Woman's Auxiliary Police Corps, to assist in the administrative duties as well as undertaking some of the duties previously regarded as those of a policeman, while as a back up there were also available recently retired men who were members of the First Police Reserve, as well as the Special Constabulary. All these, in addition to the regular officers, had also to be trained in civil defence measures, and in the course of this became closely associated with the various branches of the ARP organisation, with the result that a good foundation of efficiency and understanding was laid, aided considerably by the fact that in Bristol the Chief Constable was also in executive charge of the Wardens.

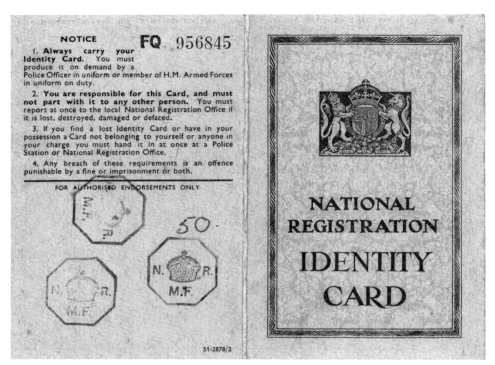

An adult's identity card. *(Author's Collection)*

Identity Cards for Everyone

On 24 August 1939 the Emergency Powers (Defence) Act was passed, a draconian measure which allowed the Government to act as it liked without reference to Parliament on matters concerning the freedom and property of any citizen simply by issuing the appropriate regulation, and three weeks after war had been declared everyone was instructed to register so that identity cards and ration books could be issued. On Friday 6 October 1939 the Emergency Committee of Bristol City Council announced that, 'Every occupier of premises in Bristol should now have received a National Registration Scheme and this should have been collected by an enumerator and identity cards issued in respect of every person who slept on the premises on the night of 29 September. If persons who have received a schedule from the enumerator or from the National Registration Office which has not been collected before tomorrow they should forward it to the National Registration Office, 136 Victoria Street, Bristol 1'. Although an essential security measure during wartime the cards, which were to be carried at all times and had to be shown on demand by members of the police or military, were retained long after the conflict had ended, and it was not until 21 February 1952 that the announcement of their abolition was made in the House of Commons, likewise the last vestiges of rationing were not removed until July 1954!

Public Information leaflets on an amazing variety of subjects were also distributed to every household in Britain, but with a lack of any enemy bombers in the skies, many people came to the conclusion that the Government had over-prepared for air attacks, and within a month polls had revealed that about half the working-class population thought that no raids would actually take place, while only a very few anticipated any heavy bombing. Nevertheless, within the first two months of war people's lives had altered dramatically following the imposition of such measures as censorship, conscription, and restrictions on lighting and even the amount of bath water that could be used, while the necessity to undertake additional war work and the shortages of food, clothing and fuel was soon putting a great strain on the whole nation.

Put That Bloody Light Out!

Although a plethora of regulations and restrictions had been introduced by the Government, of all the special measures considered necessary one of the most resented was the infamous 'blackout' introduced on the evening of 1 September 1939. This forbade the showing of any light, be it from houses, shops, factories, vehicles, street lights, or torches in the period extending from half an hour after sunset until half an hour before sunrise, in case any inadvertent chink of light showing might assist German bombers in locating their targets. At first these regulations were so strict that even lighting a cigarette in the street was a breach of the blackout as it was said that the flame of a match could be seen by an aircraft flying at 30,000ft!

To ensure compliance, householders had to install special curtains to cover the windows, and to satisfy local demand within weeks of the outbreak of war John Perris Ltd of Bridge Street, Bristol, was able to offer 'blackout' curtain casement 54in wide, at a shilling a yard, black lightproof twill 45in wide at 2s 3d a yard, and black Italian cloth 33in wide for 1s 6½d a yard. Although patrols of ARP Wardens immediately took to the streets to enforce the regulations, to begin with people tended not take the 'blackout' too seriously, and the *Bristol Evening Post* for 3 October 1939 reported that Stephen Gomm (50) of Milbrook Avenue, Brislington, had been fined 15 shillings for failing to

screen lights in his home, plus an additional 15 shillings for assaulting a special constable during an altercation between himself and the local Air Raid Warden and the policeman he had summoned to assist him! Nevertheless, Bristolians soon came to realise the importance of the 'blackout', no doubt to some extent persuaded by efforts of the city's Wardens who conducted themselves so enthusiastically that by 10 November some 248 people in Bristol had been prosecuted for breaches of the Lighting Restrictions Order.

Not surprisingly, the total darkness gave rise to a large increase in crime, and the police found it almost impossible to apprehend those responsible for the pilfering, rowdyism, wanton damage to shelters and the defacement of walls which now became common place throughout the city. Unfortunately, the 'blackout' also caused huge problems for both pedestrians and motorists alike, for not only did

crossing the street become a dangerous and hazardous business but, car drivers also suffered as all they were permitted to do to assist their passage was to use sidelights and paint the running boards and mudguards with white paint. This inevitably led to a great increase in accidents, and on 5 October the *Bristol Evening Post* told its readers that there had already been 40 road deaths in Bristol in 1939 compared with 18 in the comparable period of the previous year.

As if to highlight the problem, the following day the same paper carried the story of one unfortunate lady's demise.

> 'A "blackout" fatality was described at a Bristol inquest on Mrs Rhoda Bray (62) of 80 Gordon Road, Whitehall, who died from injuries received when she was involved in a collision with a car in Gordon Road on the nigh of 22 September. A verdict of "Accidental Death" was returned, it being stated that the night was very dark and that the deceased was dressed in dark clothes. Mr Henry George Smith, of Stanley Close, Gordon Road, said he was walking along Gordon Road at about 10 o'clock when Mrs Bray came out of her house. He bumped into her because it was practically impossible to see her. "She walked along the pavement about 12 yards, and then stepped off it to cross the road. I saw the lights of a car coming as I walked away. The next thing I heard was some glass breaking and the squealing of brakes. I do not think the motorist had the slightest chance of seeing the woman who was wearing dark clothes.'

As a result of this and similar incidents, less than a week later Bristol City Council's Emergency Committee resolved that a deputation should be sent to the Home Office urging them to relax the restrictions on lighting until the first air raids had actually taken place. This, together with similar petitions from elsewhere in the country, seems to have done the trick and in early January 1940 the authorities announced that a light intensity of 0.00025ft candles on the ground could safely be kept burning during an air raid. This permitted car headlamps to be used, provided that they were covered by a mask which threw a narrow beam of light down on to the road, while to aid pedestrians the use of masked torches was also allowed. Furthermore, the edges of pavement curbs, steps and trees growing in pavements were also daubed with white paint in an attempt to reduce accidents.

Dig For Victory and Recycle Your Waste

Once war had actually started imported food quickly became more difficult to obtain and, even though there was still just enough to go round, rationing was introduced to ensure that what was available was fairly distributed to both rich and poor alike. On 8 January 1940 the Ministry of Food began rationing bacon, ham, butter and sugar, and on 11 March meat was put on the list on the

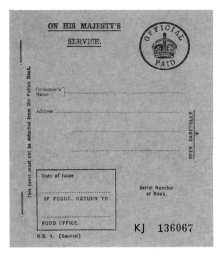

ON HIS MAJESTY'S
SERVICE.

OFFICIAL PAID

Consumer's Name

Address

OPEN CAREFULLY

Date of Issue

IF FOUND, RETURN TO

Serial Number
of Book.

FOOD OFFICE.

KJ   136067

R.B. 1. [General]

This cover must not be detached from the Ration Book.

A wartime ration book. *(Author's Collection)*

financial basis of a shillings worth a week. To this was added on 8 July, tea, cooking fats, jam and cheese, and although not actually put on ration, milk and eggs were soon being supplied to shops in proportion to the number of people they had registered. Initially people were allowed weekly rations of essential foods, and by late 1940 this amounted to a shilling's worth of meat, 8oz of sugar, an ounce of fat, an ounce of cheese and 2oz of tea. Each person had 20 points to use on whatever foodstuff they wanted most and everyone had to register with one particular shop for the weekly essential rations, although the less vital foods on the monthly points rationing could be bought from any supplier.

Substitutes for certain scarce foodstuffs were also introduced, and these included margarine for butter and saccharine for sugar, and although milk, potatoes and eggs were also sold in powdered form, many people complained about the taste, in spite of careful cooking instructions having being issued by the Ministry of Food. Beer, bread and potatoes were not rationed, although supplies could never be guaranteed, but vegetables were still fairly plentiful due to the success of the 'Dig for Victory' campaign which had resulted in so many of the city's grass verges and vacant plots of land being turned into allotments that whereas in 1939 there had been 7,782 allotment holders in Bristol, by 1943 they had mushroomed to 13,364. Individuals also cultivated vegetables in their own gardens, while open spaces in the city also went under the plough, increasing from 202 cultivated acres at the outbreak of war to 532 acres by March 1943.

With its shortage of natural resources, the country was also forced to make the best use of any materials that were available, and therefore recycling became an important part of the war effort. From 1939 onwards requests for salvage were printed in newspapers and magazines, these being designed to stir up people's enthusiasm to save a wide range of commodities. To emphasise the importance of salvage the Ministry of Supply produced impressive statistics, one advertisement claiming that 20 tons of paper would make 2,000 anti-aircraft shell containers; 20 tons of kitchen waste would feed enough pigs to produce 3,000 extra bacon rashers; 10 tons of metal would make 1,000 Bren guns; a ton of rags would make 45 airmen's dinghies, while a two ounce chop bone would fire two shots from the gun of a Hurricane fighter, feed one hen for a day, provide glue for sticking a square foot of aeroplane fabric, and fertilise a square yard of an allotment!

The need for recycling seems to have been well understood in Bristol, as during the first six months of war the materials to the value of £2,282 had been salvaged and a 'sell your iron railings' campaign had been introduced to persuade householders to hand their railings over to the Ministry of Works. Consequently, Bristol lost large quantities of these from around parks, public buildings, and private gardens, and the evidence for this can still be seen in the form of sawn off stumps along

The railings around Page Park, Staple Hill, were among many in the Bristol area lost to the salvage drive of 1940. *(Author's Collection)*

the top of many local walls. Between November 1939 and June 1940 no less than 2,348 tons of waste paper had also been collected in the city and 700 tons of redundant tram lines ripped up from its streets and taken away for scrap, while 10 tons of paper and one ton of bones were being collected each week by Bristol school children. Finally, on 10 July 1940 housewives were urged to hand in any aluminium items they might be able to spare as the metal was desperately needed for the production of aircraft. However, as by this time only about 40 per cent of the city's householders had responded to the appeal for kitchen waste, during the following month Bristol City Council began collecting such material to feed pigs and hens.

The Regional Commissioner

As early as November 1938 it had been made known that for regional control in the event of a breakdown of communications with central government the country was to be divided up into 12 regions, but it was not until May 1939 that General Sir Hugh Elles, an ex-World War One tank commander, was appointed Regional Commissioner to head the No.7 (South Western) Region, responsible for the counties of Gloucestershire, Somerset, Wiltshire, Devon and Cornwall. Each Regional Office held a headquarters comprising a Senior Regional Officer, a Treasury Officer, Regional Officers of the ARP Department, a Ministry of Health General Inspector, a Regional Police Staff Officer, a Regional Fire Officer, and liaison officers from the ministries and departments concerned. In Bristol the actual War Room was located in the cellars of numbers 19 and 21 Woodland Road, Tyndall's Park, these having been suitably equipped with steel girders, heavy metal doors, gas-filter plant, escape hatches and top priority telephone lines.

In the dark days of the early 1940s Bristolians came to have complete confidence in their Regional Commissioner and on many occasions when the wardens had been injured, or there were not enough of them, Elles arrived on the scene and took a hand in the work himself. In his farewell speech at the Council House on 28 February 1945, he declared; 'When I took office Regional Commissioners were a new invention. We started out with a very broad and indefinite mandate, so British! We were responsible for the co-operation and control of Civil Defence, and in certain circumstances responsible for the government in that part of the country to which we were appointed. What I tried to do is to boil down these two pompous words co-operation and control to two simple words, team work.'

Throughout the war Bristolians found Sir Hugh Elles easy to approach when his advice was sought, and provided that the subject had some bearing on the war, he was a good listener. Nevertheless, although he was merciless towards time wasters, he expected and inspired promptness and efficiency in those under him and was always willing to give praise when it was deserved. During the heavy raids he seemed to know instinctively where the situation was likely to be the most critical, and his appearance always brought confidence and encouragement. It was Elles's

Numbers 19 and 21 Woodland Road, Tyndall's Park, the wartime headquarters of the Regional Commissioner who headed No.7. (South-Western) Region. *(Author's Collection)*

proud boast that he never missed a single Bristol raid, and his untimely death just after the war ended was felt as a personal loss by the thousands of men and women who had served under him.

Bristol's Air Raid Precautions System

Although the Regional Commissioner headed the ARP system in his region, and Bristol was subordinated to him, the actual day to day business of dealing with ARP in the city remained in the hands of the local authority, which in the spring of 1939 appointed an ARP Controller to ensure the smooth co-operation of all Civil Defence services in the city. The man chosen to fill this position was Herbert Webb, the City Engineer, with George Gibbs, the Lord Mayor's secretary, acting as Deputy Controller. Quietly spoken and unflappable, Webb managed to do the work of several men, never lost his 'cool' and remained in the post until peace returned. To implement the local ARP organisation Bristol was divided into six Civil Defence Divisions, and north of the River Avon was created the Shirehampton Division which also took in Avonmouth Docks, the Clifton Division covering North-West Bristol, the Central Division which extended from the city centre up to Horfield, and the St George Division, which was responsible for North-East Bristol. Likewise, to the south of the Avon was the Knowle Division, covering South-East Bristol, and the Bedminster Division which looked after the South-Western part of the city.

The Control Centre, which housed the ARP Controller and his staff, was the heart of the ARP operation for it was here that, during an air raid, messages were received from the Divisional Report Centres and representatives of the essential services, such as water, electricity, gas, telephones, roads and sewers, and from where all the information required by the Regional Commissioner was passed. Originally located in very cramped quarters at Bridewell, 55 Broadmead was specially purchased to accommodate the Control Centre in September 1938, and there it remained until 11 September 1941 when the final move was made to Badminton Junior School, in Westbury on Trym. A Reserve Control Centre was also established in the tower basement of the University, and when the main Control Centre relocated to Westbury on Trym, the Reserve Control moved to Broadmead with the university being retained as a second reserve.

Later known as the Communications Service, the Report & Control Service, was the medium through which the ARP Controller exercised his power, but from the beginning the problem of personnel remained one of the most difficult, the establishment of 360 volunteers laid down by the Ministry of Home Security proving quite inadequate to staff the Divisional Report Centres in Bristol. Nevertheless, although these eventually had to rely entirely on the full-time staff by day, during the war years some 1,851 persons gave valued and faithful service to an organisation which remained on watch for 24 hours a day from the beginning of the war until the official 'Stand Down' on 2 May 1945. Information concerning an air raid incident was initially given by policemen and wardens to the appropriate Divisional Report Centre which, after collating the various messages, passed the details to its own Action Depot, as well as to the police and fire service and the city's ARP Controller, so that all interested parties would be conversant with the general situation and in a position to deal with demands for assistance.

With the outbreak of hostilities there began a period of intense activity in the organisation of the Report & Control Service, and although Bristol was unusual in making communications a unified service, the step undoubtedly had excellent results in securing co-operation and uniformity throughout the whole operational area. An important constituent of this was the Messenger Service and in the early days this was closely bound up with the Bristol Boy Scouts' Association which had been entrusted with the responsibility of organising cycle messengers, recruiting some 690 boys by September 1940, a figure later increased to about 1,000. From the first raid there was never any doubt of the value of the service, or of the courage and devotion to duty of its members, generally boys between the ages of 16 and 17, for wherever the telephones failed the Messengers carried on maintaining communications between Wardens' Posts and the Divisional Report Centres and ARP Control. Although not paid, Messengers received a small sum of money each month to cover the wear and tear of their bicycles as well as free batteries for their lamps, since much of their work was undertaken during the 'blackout' period!

The Medical and Social Services Prepare for War

In Bristol, attached to each of the Divisional Report Centres was an Action Depot from which was sent out the Rescue Parties, First Aid Parties, often accompanied by ambulances and, if required, the Gas Decontamination Squads. The task of organising and directing the Rescue Service and Gas Decontamination Squads in Bristol was undertaken by the City Engineer and Surveyor, and of the 1,050 men who initially volunteered, a total of 748 were mobilised between 2 and 4 September 1939, divided into Heavy Rescue parties of nine men and Light Rescue parties and Gas Decontamination squads of seven men each. Working alongside these were First Aid Parties, and as the idea of forming these had originated some months before hostilities commenced, between March and September 1939 everyone trained and ready for first aid duties had been allocated to units near their own homes. Consequently, First Aid Parties, which were part of the Casualty Service, were able to take their places 'en bloc' at the Action Depots when the Luftwaffe started its attacks and so render assistance at the site of an incident and to clear the area of wounded persons in the shortest possible time.

As well as the First Aid Parties and ambulances, by October 1940 the Casualty Services, headed by the city's Medical Officer of Health, had responsibility for the three Casualty Receiving Hospitals, seven Fixed First Aid Posts, 10 Mobile Units, six Cleansing Stations and six Mortuaries, while by mid-1942 some 14 First Aid Points had also been set up and a further six Gas Cleansing Stations provided.

The Casualty Receiving Hospitals for the seriously wounded of Bristol were Southmead, the Bristol Royal Infirmary and the Bristol General Hospital, while the Cossham Memorial Hospital on the edge of Kingswood was also earmarked to receive casualties from parts of East Bristol and adjoining parts of South Gloucestershire. During the period of heavy raiding in which there were a large number of seriously wounded cases, many much needed beds in the these establishments were quickly freed by the evacuation, to out-lying Base Hospitals, of all patients who could be safely moved. For this purpose use was made of a number of institutions and hospitals in adjoining counties, including the Royal West of England Sanatorium at Weston-super-Mare, the Birmingham Hospital Saturday Fund Home at Kewstoke and Eastern House School. Distributions of fracture and

Training for rescue work. *(NFS)*

other patients were also made to St Martin's Hospital at Bath, and Winford Orthopaedic Hospital in Somerset, while St Monica's Home in Bristol gave up half their number of beds to replace those lost by the Bristol Royal Infirmary. In anticipation of the German bombers returning for a second winter onslaught, in 1941 Bristol Corporation also extended the existing sanatorium at Frenchay Park to act as an Emergency Hospital to take air raid casualties, but fortunately it was never needed for that purpose.

At the start of war women volunteers trained in anti-gas work, First Aid and home nursing, together with older men recruited for First Aid duties, were allocated to the Fixed First Aid Posts located in health centres and hospitals. Their function was to receive lightly wounded cases immediately after a raid and to continue their treatment in the following days, thereby relieving congestion at the Receiving Hospitals. These proved to be so successful that by the end of the war there were eight such posts, and it was here that the Mobile Units were also housed. Each of these, staffed by a doctor, trained nurse and six auxiliary nurses, consisted of a large van containing surgical and medical equipment which could be sent to the site of a serious incident, making it possible to set up a dressing station with a minimum of delay.

Although never actually used by the Germans, the possibility still had to be considered that an attack might be made using chemical agents such as eye, nose and lung irritant gases, and skin blistering agents like Mustard Gas and Lewisite, and precautions taken to combat the effects. The first line of defence was to be the gas mask, various varieties of which were manufactured to suit the emergency services, adult civilians, children and babies. Their issue to the population of Bristol

Hitler will send no warning – so always carry your gas mask

ISSUED BY THE MINISTRY OF HOME SECURITY

began on 30 September 1938, and although initially the respirators, as they were officially known, were in short supply, during February and March 1939 mass distribution took place from a number of depots set up around the city. Although most people carried their gas masks with them during the first few weeks after war had been declared, by November 1939 and in spite of an intense advertising campaign, relatively few people were bothering to carry them when venturing out onto the streets.

Nevertheless, had the unthinkable actually happened and gas bombs been employed against Bristol, the presence of the substance first had to be confirmed by the local Gas Identification Officer after which persons who might have been in touch with gas, but were not seriously injured, would have been sent to one of the Public Cleansing Stations installed in six of the city's public baths. Later, due to official concerns that the Germans might resort to the use of gas during any Allied landings on the Continent, Bristol's Decontamination Service was extended by the construction of additional cast concrete Cleansing Stations in areas of dense population.

Finally, for those who unfortunately lost their lives during an attack, six Divisional Mortuaries were provided in Bristol and these came into action after each raid, that in the Central Division also being ear-marked as a Gas Decontamination Centre for the dead. After major attacks, during which whole families might perish together, the provision of burial also became a problem, and this resulted in a number of the victims being laid to rest in communal graves in Greenbank Cemetery, the interments usually being carried out amidst the expressions of silent sympathy, much more expressive than any spoken word.

The city fathers, however, were quick to voice the feelings of many Bristolians, and after their first experience of heavy bombing the Lord Mayor spoke on their behalf.

'Those who have fallen have paid the supreme sacrifice for the honour of their city', he said, 'Bravely did these valiant hearts bear themselves. Many heroes fell in the act of duty and service for their fellow men, with no thought of self, but bravely carrying on their work of protection and rescue. Parents

Anti-gas training. *(NFS)*

Jacob's Wells Baths, Jacob's Wells Road, were used as a special cleansing station for the Clifton ARP division during World War Two. *(Author's Collection)*

and children united in family life were in death not divided. Innocent children were massacred, as of old, at the feet of tyranny. To the honour and sacred memory of them all we bow our heads today in loving gratitude. "From the rising of the sun till the going down of the same we will remember them". To those relatives and friends who mourn their loss, on behalf of this Council and our city, I express our sincerest sympathy. To them I would say, "Side by side with you we mourn your loss and share your sorrow. We pray that in this hour of your great need and abundance of God's gracious love and mercy may be vouchsafed to you and give you comfort. Your city owes your loved ones and you a debt of gratitude which can never be fully paid. We will honour them and you by every endeavour to be worthy of the sacrifice they have made". Our praise cannot be too high, our gratitude cannot be too deep, our love cannot be too abounding, our practical sympathy and help cannot be too generous.'

Not only was assistance given to the relatives of those who had paid the ultimate price, but provision also had to be made for the other survivors of the air-raids, particularly those who were suffering the greatest degree of hardship. As a first step towards overcoming this problem, in 1939 the Bristol City Council had asked religious organisations and voluntary helpers to collaborate and to undertake the care of people rendered destitute or homeless as a result of the bombing. Under

The memorial archway leading to Bristol's civilian war graves in Greenbank Cemetery. The right hand stone tablet reads: 'To the memory of those civilians who lost their lives in this city through enemy action in the world war of 1939–1945'. *(Author's Collection)*

the inspiring leadership of the Dean of Bristol, the Very Revd H.W. Blackburne, the Voluntary Hostel Committee was set up, and this organisation, composed of clergy and members of all religious denominations went on to establish some 77 hostels in such places as church halls and schools, and these were subsequently equipped by the city's Social Welfare Committee.

That then was the basic framework within which the whole civil defence system was supposed to operate, but in the stress of the 'Night Blitz' the organisation sometimes became overstressed, in which case the ordinary ARP workers had to make on the spot decisions and often extemporise. Fortunately for Bristol, enemy activity started in a fairly subdued manner and the small nuisance raids of the summer of 1940 were exactly what the civil defence services

required to hone the organisation to a high level of efficiency, enabling it to perform with great professionalism when the bombing started in earnest in the winter of 1940–41.

CHAPTER 2

DEFENCES INSTALLED AND OPERATIONAL

June 1938 to July 1940

During January 1939 the Government published *National Service. A Guide To The Ways In Which The Peoples Of This Country May Give Service*, and this gives a good insight into the way in which people were beginning to see the situation as conflict in Europe edged ever nearer. 'We have no thought of aggression: our one wish is to live at peace with all peoples. But if this wish is to be fulfilled we must be up and doing. We must make ourselves strong so that our influence for peace be real, and we must make ourselves safe so that others cannot be tempted to thoughts of aggression against us'.

This having been said, the first step towards providing air defences for the area had in fact been taken back in 1937 when the headquarters of No.23 Observer Corps Group was established in Bristol. By June 1938 this formation, the principal task of which was the plotting and identification of enemy aircraft over land, had set up some 33 Observer Posts covering Bristol, North Somerset, South Gloucestershire and Wiltshire. The Corps also provided information from which Fighter Command initiated the Air Raid Warnings throughout the country, and in April 1941 received the title 'Royal' in recognition of the valuable work it was undertaking, often by men working in long hours in posts in exposed locations with little protection from the elements and with no opportunity to light a fire which might be seen from the air.

In September 1938 the government announced that balloon barrage protection was to be provided for a number of provincial towns and cities including Bristol, where it was decided that the presence of Filton aerodrome prevented the use of balloons to cover the whole area. Two small independent layouts were therefore proposed, one to protect the harbour installations at Avonmouth and Portishead and the other the Bristol City Docks. The system involved raising a lethal cable barrage into the air around the potential target compelling an enemy bomber to fly above the balloons at heights at which other anti-aircraft weapons could be used against it more effectively, and from which it would bomb less accurately.

The balloons employed were flown from a mobile winch and were designed to be deployed at a maximum altitude of 5,000ft, although when the barrage area was not directly threatened the balloons were grounded or kept close hauled at 500ft to provide as little potential danger as possible to 'friendly' aircraft. Provincial barrages were initially organised into Auxiliary Air Force Squadrons operating some 24 balloons each. In each locality depots, known as Balloon Centres, were formed to administer the balloon squadrons and to be responsible for the assembly and testing of balloons

A surviving squadron office in front of two original fabric shops on Pucklechurch Trading Estate, previously the site of No.11 Balloon Centre. *(Author's Collection)*

and the training of balloon crews in time of war. In the Bristol area February 1939 saw the start of recruiting for the three 'County of Gloucester' Squadrons, No.927, 928 and 929, with these moving to Pucklechurch on 9 August when the new camp was taken over as the permanent home for the local No.11 Balloon Centre, which in turn was responsible to RAF Balloon Command.

By late 1938 it had become obvious to the War Office that recruiting for their new anti-aircraft and searchlight formations was not proceeding fast enough, and so they asked for existing Territorial Army units of other rôles and other arms to accept conversion to anti-aircraft duties. Consequently, in Bristol at the beginning of November 1938 the 66th (South Midland) Field Brigade took over heavy anti-aircraft duties, becoming the 76th Heavy Anti-Aircraft Regiment, while the 4th (City of Bristol) Battalion, The Gloucestershire Regiment, was re-designated the 66th Searchlight Regiment. Nevertheless, although this went some way towards solving the manning problem, at the outbreak of war heavy anti-aircraft guns for the close defence of potential targets in Britain were in very short supply as the first production model of the new and improved Vickers 3.7" gun with an effective engagement ceiling of 25,000ft had only appeared in early 1938. Although some of the lower performance 3" 20 cwt. semi-mobile guns were available as a stop-gap measure, these were essentially little more than a World War One weapon on a modified carriage, with an effective ceiling of only 14,000ft.

Because of the shortages, initially only four-gun positions were built, although at airfields two guns were considered acceptable, while until suitable gun-laying radar became available, action with any degree of accuracy was only possible against visible targets, otherwise blind barrages were all that could be fired by the gunners. To assist the guns and fighter aircraft an elaborate searchlight layout was prepared for Southern England, with each major Gun Defended Area, such as Bristol, being provided with a local system to provide illumination for night engagements, the projectors being deployed in groups of 48 on a 3,500yd spacing. By late 1939 improved sound locators to operate in conjunction with the searchlights had also been introduced, and apart from directing the searchlight beams the new locators were also used to assist the Army's Anti-Aircraft Command with the plotting of night raids.

Light anti-aircraft guns were also provided to give protection from attacks carried out at altitudes of less than 3,000ft against certain important installations known as 'Vulnerable Points', and these included the Bristol Aeroplane Company's factory at Filton, Filton Aerodrome, the Imperial Smelting's zinc plant at Avonmouth, the Corporation's electricity generating station at Portishead and Parnall Aircraft at Yate. In December 1938 the 23rd Light Anti-Aircraft Regiment was formed at Bristol to which a number of Territorial Army Reserve personnel were recruited, resulting, at the outbreak of war, in the guns often being manned by shifts of workers on sites near their places of employment. However, due to a severe lack of personnel and equipment many of the sites allocated to the regiment were initially occupied by men from heavy, rocket and searchlight batteries, and it was to be May 1940 before the situation was anything like being resolved, although the provision of adequate weapons remained a problem for several years.

Originally it had been assumed that 0.303" Lewis guns would be adequate, but it was soon realised that a more specialised weapon would be necessary. The mobile single-barrel Swedish Bofors 40mm gun was selected as the ideal equipment, but due to manufacturing problems it was 1942 before production overtook demand. In an attempt to rectify this situation during the first three years of war the shortfall was mainly made up by using Vickers Mark VIII naval two-pounders with specially designed land mountings, old World War One 3" heavy anti-aircraft guns fitted with deflection sights, and Hispano 20mm cannons, although all of these proved to be far from ideal.

At the beginning of December 1938 Bristol's own No.501 (County of Gloucester) Squadron, Auxiliary Airforce, at that time flying

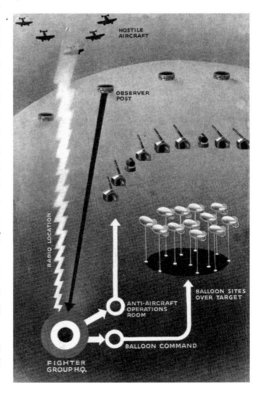

This chart showing Britain's air defence system was released to the public in 1943. *(Official Photograph)*

bombers from Filton airfield was finally re-designated a fighter squadron with a complement of some twenty pilots and sixteen aircraft, twelve of which were to be at operational readiness in time of war to take part in the defence of the Bristol area. The squadron's first Hawker Hurricane arrived in early March 1939, and this was one of two similar single engined monoplane fighters available to the RAF at the outbreak of war, both of which were armed with eight machine guns. The Hurricane, which was a very stable gun platform well suited to destroying bombers, had a maximum speed of around 330mph, while the Supermarine Spitfire, the most advanced of the single engined interceptors available at the time, was able to fly at over 350mph.

So it was that by mid-August 1939 the main components of the country's air defences were assembled under RAF Fighter Command which for operational purposes was divided into a number of geographical Groups, each sub-divided into Sectors. The Sector Operations Room at Filton was responsible not only for the RAF's locally based fighters and the balloon barrage, but also for Anti-Aircraft Command's searchlights and anti-aircraft guns, which in the Bristol area were controlled from the Army's Gun Operations Room at Worrall Road in Clifton.

The Sector Operations Room also received information about the movement of hostile aircraft from the Observer Corps and the searchlight sites, while at the same time maintaining direct communication with adjacent Sectors and Groups, as well as with Fighter Command headquarters.

General Mobilisation

Meanwhile, on 24 August, the general mobilisation scheme had begun to be put into operation, as a result of which the balloon squadrons started leaving Pucklechurch to occupy their wartime sites, forming skeleton barrages around the vital port facilities at Avonmouth and Bristol. In the next few months, however, two of the squadrons were transferred to Eastern England where their services were more urgently required leaving only No.927 Squadron to man both the both local barrages. Although a replacement unit was formed at Pucklechurch in December during the winter of 1939–40 balloon production was unable to keep pace with demand, so it was to be the end of March before the new unit, No.951 Squadron, was finally declared operational.

The army's heavy anti-aircraft guns had also moved to their war stations by early September 1939, and although initially operating from temporary sites, by late November were emplaced on permanent positions at Easton in Gordano, Portishead, Rockingham near Avonmouth, Cribbs Causeway, Brickfields at Winterbourne, and on Purdown. During the ensuing months the mobile guns were exchanged for statics and by the beginning of June 1940 four 3.7" weapons were in place on each of the sites providing the Bristol area with a total of 24 heavy anti-aircraft guns with which to counter the expected raids, far too few as it turned out for so important a target.

Following mobilisation light anti-aircraft guns were also set up at the Portishead power station, the Parnall Aircraft plant at Yate and the Bristol Aeroplane Company's premises at Filton. In addition heavy anti-aircraft and searchlight units also installed anti-aircraft machine guns around the local docks. In Bristol they were placed on the Wills Factory, Co-operative Wholesale Society Building, the bonded warehouses at Canon's Marsh and Cumberland Basin and on the Bristol Food Concerns premises, while at Avonmouth the guns were set up at the smelting works. However, these were to be short term deployments, the guns all being removed by early 1940 when balloon barrages effectively covered these locations. Although the original plan had been to deploy searchlights at intervals of 3,500yd, due to a shortage of money at the outbreak of war only about half the equipment necessary had been delivered forcing a 6,000yd spacing in many places. Because of this, by early October only 24 searchlights had been deployed in the Bristol Gun Defended Area, and it was to be June 1940 before anything approaching the full complement was in place.

In spite of being a home posting life in Anti-Aircraft Command was much more difficult than had been generally imagined, particularly by the rest of the Army, as the men tended to be deployed in small groups all over the country, many of them under junior NCO's and miles from the nearest habitation and any form of entertainment. As heavy AA gun and searchlight sites were desolate places, the life of the gunners and operators tended to be lonely and monotonous and after the declaration of war as men had then to be in constant readiness 24 hours a day, some who had been on duty all night found themselves carrying out maintenance work during the day. To compound the misery the first winter of war was not easy for the men, many of whom were still in temporary accommodation, as snow fell early in December, and about Christmas time a severe frost set in which held well into February causing great hardship to all working on exposed positions. Furthermore for the first nine months of war no gunners or searchlight operators in the Bristol area had a chance to engage a German aircraft so it became progressively more important to keep the men busy all day with training maintenance, physical training, arms drill, fatigues and construction work on the camp, for without the incentive of an enemy efficiency could rapidly decline.

A general view of the Command & Control centre on the Purdown gun site. *(Author's Collection)*

The surviving Magazine on the Purdown heavy anti-aircraft gun site. *(Author's Collection)*

Scramble the Fighters!

A Hawker Hurricane IIc's of No.87 Squadron at Charmy Down. *(via G. Morley)*

Not surprisingly, the only local defenders to see any action during the Phoney War were the pilots of RAF Fighter Command, and their chance finally came on 10 November 1939 when No.501 Squadron was scrambled in an unsuccessful attempt to intercept a German reconnaissance aircraft which had been reported in the Gloucester area, the honour of being the first pilot to take-off in the defence of Bristol going to Flight Lieutenant E.S. Williams, flying Hurricane L2055. This, however, was an isolated incident and as there was now more enemy activity over South Eastern England the unit moved to that area later that month. A squadron of obsolete Gloster Gladiator biplane fighters replaced them, but these only remained at Filton until April 1940 when No.263 Squadron was hurriedly dispatched to Norway in a futile attempt to halt the German invasion.

The Bristol Areoplane Company's works at Filton from the air. *(BAC)*

This lack of fighter protection alarmed Sir Stanley White, the Managing Director of the Bristol Aeroplane Company, and on 27 May he wrote to Fighter Command requesting that a balloon barrage should be provided to protect the company's works at Filton, although he was well aware of the difficulties this might cause to any aircraft operating from the nearby aerodrome. The response was rapid and two days later White was informed that he would get his balloons, No. 935 Squadron moving immediately from Cardiff to Filton. Because of this, from the end of May until late September only a few fighter squadrons were on short term deployment at Filton as the balloon barrage had made the airfield difficult to use as a fighter station by day, and impossible by night.

The German attack on France and the Low Countries on 10 May 1940, brought the 'Phoney War' to a rapid conclusion and caused frantic efforts to be made to spread Britain's fighter defence westward. The first new airfield to be occupied was Middle Wallop, in Hampshire which, lying some six miles south-west of Andover, was ideally sited to intercept enemy aircraft bound for Bristol, the majority of which would have to come in over Lyme Bay. 1 June saw the first Hurricanes from No. 601 Squadron arrive, to be followed in the middle of the month by the stop-gap and totally inadequate twin-engined Bristol Blenheim night fighters of No. 236 Squadron, some of which were even fitted with the new Airborne Interception radar, although this equipment was still of relatively low performance and very unreliable.

The Real Dad's Army

Now for the first time a real threat of invasion hung over Britain, and in response on 14 May Anthony Eden, Secretary of State for War, broadcast in appeal for men to defend the country in which he said that:

> 'We want large numbers to come forward now and offer their services. The name of the new
> force will be the Local Defence Volunteers. When on duty you will form part of the Armed
> Forces and your period of service will be for the duration of the war.'

Three days later the LDV achieved legal status with the passing of a Defence (Local Defence Volunteers) Order in Council, and the following day the War Office issued instructions to Command and Area Headquarters explaining that the volunteers were to be organised into sections, platoons and companies, but that LDV organisers and leaders would not hold commissions or have the power to command regular forces. Although Eden had mentioned in his broadcast that the men 'would receive uniform and will be armed' the War Office let it be known that for the time being only arm-bands with L.D.V stencilled on them would be available until khaki denim two-piece overalls and extra service caps could be manufactured in sufficient quantities.

After the broadcast, men between the ages of 17 and 65 flocked in their hundreds to police stations throughout Bristol to fill in their application forms, and Major Clifford and Captain Talbot-Plumb, having sworn each other in, set about the task of raising units of the LDV for service in the city. Concerned captains of industry also began to encourage their workers to organise special factory defence units, and of the six companies initially formed in Bristol one was recruited from the employees of the Bristol Aeroplane Company, and another made up of men working at Avonmouth Docks, while each of the remaining four units was raised in an existing Police Division.

On 17 June the Territorial Army Association took over the administration of the LDV, and two days later Lieutenant Colonel A.F. Chapman was appointed the commander of the Bristol LDV Corps. Recruiting had been so fast that companies in some parts of the country soon numbered as many as 2,000 men, so on 1 July they were re-designated battalions, while still retaining the name of the town or city in which they had been raised. Locally, this resulted in 'A' Company covering North-Central Bristol becoming No.1 Battalion, 'B' Company covering South Bristol becoming No.2 Battalion, and 'C' Company covering West Bristol becoming No.3 Battalion. Likewise, 'D' Company in East Bristol became No.4 Battalion, and 'E' Company in Filton and Patchway became No.5 Battalion, while 'S' Company in Avonmouth and Shirehampton was re-designated No.6 Battalion. At the same time the command structure was revised and the country divided into Zones, and locally this ensured that Lieutenant Colonel Chapman was appointed Bristol Zone Commander, a position that was to give him much of the responsibility for the ground defences of the city.

To begin with each company confined its activities to its own particular locality where, from dawn to dusk, it manned observation posts, watched for airborne invasions, provided road patrols, constructed road blocks in order to screen traffic and prevent parachute troops from entering the city, and furnished guards for important buildings and vital points. Although weapons for the LDV were slow in coming every form of improvisation was adopted and shot guns, pikes and home made grenades were plentiful, keenness and enthusiasm making up for the rest! Nevertheless, by the second week of July supplies of World War One vintage rifles from Canada and the United States were being distributed to LDV units all over Britain, while in his radio broadcast on 14 July Winston Churchill, the Prime Minister, remarked that the LDV would be better described as the Home Guard, a name which was officially sanctioned on 31 July, while the Home Guard's role as part of the British Army was officially ratified on 6 August. With the original companies having been upgraded to battalions, rank style and symbolism followed shortly after, and during September the local formations were re-designated City of Bristol Battalions of the Home Guard.

Hitler's Luftwaffe

As the process of re-armament had gathered pace during the second half of the 1930s the local aircraft industry in particular had expanded rapidly, so that by the end of 1939 the Bristol Aeroplane Company was the single largest aircraft manufacturing unit in the world, their buildings at Filton and Patchway covering 2½ million sq ft. Here were to be produced mainly Blenheims, Beauforts, Beaufighters and Buckingham's, together with such engines as the Taurus, Perseus and Hercules. Likewise, five miles to east-north-east at Yate, Parnall Aircraft, the main production centre for the Frazer-Nash gun turrets fitted in most British bombers, later went on to become an important Spitfire sub-frame contractor. Consequently, when the bombing campaign began the aircraft manufacturing plants at Filton and Yate, as well as the Avonmouth, Portishead and Bristol City docks and their associated industries and utilities, all became prime targets for the Luftwaffe.

In fact, so strategically important was the area that between October 1938 and January 1943 the German Air Force's intelligence branch busied themselves issuing information folders on about 50 individual military, industrial and commercial objectives in and around Bristol, which contained not

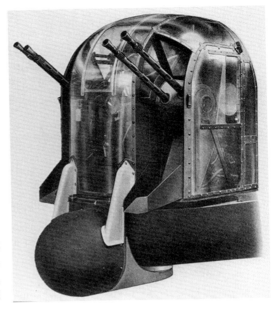

The Frazer Nash FN121 turret, manufactured by Parnall Aircraft at Yate and fitted to RAF Lancaster bombers. (*Creda*)

only photographs and descriptions, but also detailed maps which were nothing more than rescaled and annotated copies of those produced by the British Ordnance Survey! In an attempt to obtain up to date photographic coverage, even before the outbreak of war the Luftwaffe High Command's strategic reconnaissance unit, the Aufkl. Gr. Ob. d. L., had been engaged in clandestine photographic work using military aircraft carrying civilian markings, and early on the afternoon of 29 August, potential targets at Yate were photographed during such a sortie.

By the summer of 1940 the German bombers the slowly evolving British air defences were expected to engage were all twin-engined machines, for by that time the Luftwaffe was operating the Dornier Do 17 capable of carrying a 1,000kg bomb load, together with the Heinkel He 111, and the newly introduced Junkers Ju 88, both with a 2,000kg capability. The Messerschmitt Bf 110 long-range escort fighter, which at times was used as a light bomber, also saw limited service during the late summer, but its operations were usually confined to daylight precision attacks.

Although German aircraft had been engaging the Royal Navy in its anchorages in Scotland, as well as carrying out aerial minelaying off the English east coast since October 1939, throughout the 'Phoney War' the Luftwaffe had held back from attacking mainland Britain, and even its overflying reconnaissance missions had ceased by mid-January 1940. However, following the invasion of France RAF bombers began raiding industrial installations in the Ruhr, and this enraged Hitler who on 24 May issued a directive authorising the Luftwaffe to start attacking Britain as soon as sufficient forces became available. The prime objectives were to be important docks, such as Avonmouth, as well as key points of the aircraft industry and other industrial plants vital to the war effort. Nevertheless, all remained quiet until in mid-June when, with the fall of France imminent, the two significant German air fleets on the Western Front, Luftflotte 2 and Luftflotte 3, began occupying newly overrun aerodromes, the former in Northern France and the Low Countries, and the latter in France west of the River Seine, thus bringing the Bristol area at last within reach of fully loaded German bombers.

These Luftflotten were, in fact, self-contained mini-airforces each provided with their own individually controlled fighter, bomber and reconnaissance elements, and by early July spheres of

The Heinkel He 111H medium bomber. *(via G. Morley)*

operation had become clearly defined, with Luftflotte 2 being allocated targets in Eastern England, and Luftflotte 3 those on the western side of the country. This latter formation was made up of the bomber units KG 27 and KG 55 which flew Heinkel 111s, and KG 51 and LG 1 operating Junkers 88s, a type to which KG 54 was also in the process of converting, and although between them they possessed around 500 aircraft, about a quarter would be unserviceable at any one time. With each airfleet assigned its own objectives, for the next six months Luftflotte 3 alone undertook attacks on the Bristol area, the only exception being the odd bomb dropped locally by I./KG 4 and KGr 126, Luftflotte 2's minelaying formations, which were excluded from the geographical constraints.

To begin with, the high-explosive bombs employed by the Luftwaffe in operations over the Bristol area were exclusively of the 50 and 250kg types, with the smaller bomb predominating. However, during September 1940 weapons of increasing size and weight began to come into service, and by the end of November not only had 500kg bombs been dropped locally, but also a smaller number of the heavy 1,000, 1,400, 1,700, and 1,800kg varieties. Although the available high

The Junkers Ju 88A medium bomber. *(via G. Morley)*

explosives possessed great destructive power, perhaps the most potent of German bombs remained the tiny 1kg magnesium incendiary which were dropped in profusion and caused millions of pounds worth of fire damage to British cities. Bristol was no exception and these incendiaries were largely responsible for raising to the ground large parts of central area, destroying irreplaceable medieval buildings and changing the cityscape for ever. Although

The Dornier Do 17Z medium bomber. *(via G. Morley)*

A chart showing the different types of high-explosive bomb dropped on Bristol between 1940 and 1944. *(Author's Collection)*

A drawing of the B1 El, the standard German 1kg incendiary bomb. *(Author's Collection)*

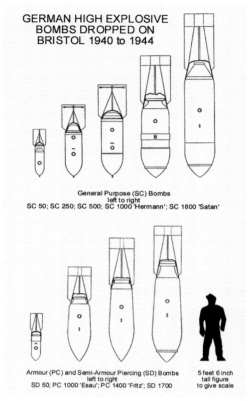

GERMAN HIGH EXPLOSIVE BOMBS DROPPED ON BRISTOL 1940 to 1944

General Purpose (SC) Bombs
left to right
SC 50; SC 250; SC 500; SC 1000 'Hermann'; SC 1800 'Satan'

Armour (PC) and Semi-Armour Piercing (SD) Bombs
left to right
SD 50; PC 1000 'Esau'; PC 1400 'Fritz'; SD 1700

5 feet 6 inch tall figure to give scale

these devices burnt with a heat sufficient to melt steel, in an attempt to deter the fire-fighters and spread the burning magnesium more effectively, from late November 1940 the Germans began dropping small numbers of 'explosive incendiaries' on Bristol, these being similar to the standard bomb, but with a small charge fitted under the tail which detonated two minutes after impact. Another weapon deployed against Bristol from late June 1940 until January 1941 was the large, but somewhat unreliable, incendiary device known in Britain as the 'oil bomb' as it contained an oil mixture and a high-explosive bursting charge contained within a thin casing of similar size to a standard 250kg high explosive.

Bristol's Baptism of Fire

At first German air operations over Britain were carried out on a small scale, and these began with light probing raids by night, normally carried out by as few as five aircraft against a single target. These harassing attacks were, in the months that followed, directed against specific targets such as aircraft factories, dock installations, oil storage tanks, specialised manufacturing plants and airfields. Regular operations against Britain commenced on 18 June 1940 when, using a newly captured French aerodrome, Luftwaffe night bombers began targeting Bomber Command airfields in Eastern England, only a matter of hours after the local Sector Station at Filton had assumed temporary responsibility for three new fighter airfields which had just received their first operational units. This force comprised one squadron of Hurricanes, No.213 at Exeter, and two of Spitfires, No.92 based at Pembrey, near Swansea, in South Wales, and No.234 down at St Eval, in Cornwall, all put in place to protect the approaches to Bristol, South Wales and the industrial Midlands.

Hours later, on the night of 19 June, the first Luftwaffe bombers took off on missions to the West Country, the Bristol Aeroplane Company at Filton and the docks at Avonmouth and Southampton being the objective for about seven Heinkel 111s from I./KG 27 flying from

25 June 1940. The first-high explosive bomb dropped on Bristol fell here at the junction of Lower Maudlin Street, killing an elderly man and woman. *(Jim Facey)*

Merville airfield near the Franco-Belgian border. Unfortunately for them navigation over 'blacked-out' England proved more difficult than expected, and although one of the returning crews subsequently claimed to have seen bombs impact on the wharf and a flak installation at Avonmouth, in reality the high explosives fell harmlessly along the shore at Portishead, where some ten were reported at 2.12am. Nevertheless, in spite of this somewhat inauspicious start the war was about come to Bristol, and later that day the German radio made this abundantly clear when it announced that;

> 'The oil storage tanks in Hull, Bristol, one of the greatest English trading and free cities, and Southampton, the transatlantic port, have been bombed. The revenge of the German Air Force for England's sly night piracy has begun. German forbearance is exhausted. The time for settlement has come.'

This was no idle threat, and the next operation against the area was undertaken on the night of 24 June, during which the crews of five Heinkel 111s from I./KG 27 that had been briefed to raid the Bristol Aeroplane Company's plant claimed to have successfully attacked it with 720 incendiaries and sixty 50kg bombs. This, however, was another case of wishful thinking, as at 12.17am small incendiaries began falling in the St Philip's district of Bristol, followed shortly after by a high-explosive bomb which impacted at the corner of Lower Maudlin Street and Harford Street, quite close to the centre of the city, where it killed Mary Stinchcombe and Frederick Meek, the first innocent victims of the Luftwaffe's bombing campaign against the West Country. A little under an hour later incendiaries and high explosives also came down in the Brislington area, where at Glenarm Walk a mother, her young daughter, and a close neighbour, all lost their lives. Unlike on the previous occasion, the RAF were in a position to attempt to intercept the enemy, and during the course of this attack Blenheim L6904, flown by Squadron Leader P.E. Drew and Pilot Officer B. Nokes-Cooper from No.236 Squadron at Middle Wallop, became the first night fighter to take part, albeit unsuccessfully, in the defence of Bristol when it became airborne just after midnight to patrol near Shaftesbury.

Unfortunately, due to the strict censorship imposed, the local newspapers

The corner of Lower Maudlin Street and Deep Street is now covered by part of the Bristol Eye Hospital. *(Author's Collection)*

Damage to 14 Glenarm Walk, Brislington, following the raid of 24 June. A mother and her nine year old daughter lost their loves here. *(BUP)*

were unable to give any anything but vague details of where the raid took place, although some 48 hours later the *Western Daily Press* was permitted to publish the names of those killed and injured.

'Five dead, 14 seriously injured, and many suffering from cuts and minor injuries. That is the casualty list of Monday night's air raid on a south-west town, when high explosives and incendiary bombs were dropped, fires started and damage done to private houses. The following were killed – Mrs Noel and her daughter Rosina (9), Hubert Goodwin (37), Frederick Meek (65), and Mrs Mary Stinchcombe (67). Seriously injured Miss V. De Santis, Miriam De Santis, Rosina Franklin, William Franklin, Eliza Harris (82), George Saunders (41), Florence Stinchcombe (29), Charles Wintle (41), Ellen Whatley (47), Horace Wide (18), and Jack Watts (24). Reports received from various centres state that Bancroft is in a critical condition, but that the rest of the casualties are "going on well", "fairly comfortable", and "improving".'

Today 14 Glenarm Walk, Brislington, shows no signs of wartime damage. *(Author's Collection)*

A 3.7in mobile Anti-Aircraft gun. *(Author's Collection)*

'The alarm was sounded at about 12.15am and the all-clear went some hours later. Most of the damage was done in a district that is almost entirely residential. A number of bombs were dropped. Four houses were almost completely demolished, and many houses in the area had windows blown out and slates torn from the roofs. Mrs Noel and Miss Rosina Noel were killed when a bomb fell in their front garden, blowing-out the entire front of the house. It is believed that they were standing at their front door at the time. Mr Hubert Goodwin, who lived on the opposite side of the road, was also killed, apparently by a bomb splinter, while Mr. Reginald Bancroft, another neighbour, is in a local hospital suffering from severe injuries.'

Up until then cloud cover had prevented the local heavy anti-aircraft guns from going into action against the raiders, but just before midnight on the 26 the Cribbs site became the first in the Bristol Gun Defended Area to fire in anger, the men of 237 Battery, 76th HAA Regiment expending two rounds during the course of a nuisance attack aimed at Avonmouth and Portishead Docks by two crews from KG 27. With the bombing campaign now under way the Luftwaffe also embarked on a comprehensive photographic reconnaissance of Britain, the first sortie over Bristol being undertaken on 29 June by a Heinkel 111 of the Aufkl Gr Ob.d.L. They were joined in this work early the following month by the reconnaissance element of Luftflotte 3 and the assorted Junkers 88s, Dornier 17s and Messerschmitt 110s of 3.(F)/31, 4.(F)/14, 3. and 4.(F)/121 and 1.,2. and 3.(F)/123 went on to fly regular photo-reconnaissance sorties over the area until the winter of 1940 when the strengthened British defences forced them to restrict their activities to immediate pre and post-raid coverage missions.

Although by late June German daylight sorties had started to prove vulnerable when confronted by Hurricanes or Spitfires, they had little to fear from the unsuitably equipped fledgling night fighter force. Nevertheless, in spite of the RAF's resources being stretched to the limit, an effort was made to provide some additional form of protection to Britain's vital factories, ports, and industrial installations, by instructing the local day fighter squadrons to provide aircraft to fly radarless 'Cats Eye' patrols at night. As a result, a small detachment of fighters was sent each evening to Hullavington, a flying training station located some five miles north of Chippenham, from where the first patrol by two of No.92 Squardon's Spitfires was undertaken early on the morning of 1 July. Nevertheless, in spite of the sterling efforts made by the pilots flying these sorties accidents were not uncommon, and to add to the problems the Hurricanes and Spitfires employed were virtually

Bristol–Avonmouth, grain silos and large mill of the Co-Operative Wholesale Co., target GB 56 64. Document b, the photograph, taken at about 9.30am on the morning of 29 June 1940 by an aircraft from Aufklärungsgruppe Ob.d.L. and issued in April 1941.

useless at night unless the target was silhouetted against cloud, so it was nothing less than pure chance if a fighter arrived in the right place at the right time.

Harassing attacks against local targets were now being undertaken almost every night, and the air war intensified further on 2 July when the Luftwaffe received instructions to gain and maintain air superiority over the English Channel, something it quickly achieved. The victory, however, was tactical rather

The Spitfire I. Although an excellent day fighter, its narrow undercarriage caused it to be quickly withdrawn from night operations. *(via G. Morley)*

than strategic, because Britain's seaborne communications with the world were uninterrupted, the ships being loaded and discharged at ports on the western coast, difficult and dangerous for the Luftwaffe to reach in daylight. The harbour facilities such as those at Bristol and Avonmouth, Newport, Cardiff, Swansea, Liverpool, and Glasgow now assumed great importance to the British economy, and night attacks against them, as well as the local aircraft industry, continued throughout the summer, the Bristol, Avonmouth and Portishead docks complex, as well as the Bristol Aeroplane Company, each being targeted about twenty times between mid-June and the end of August.

Although the damage caused by these early nocturnal raids was only slight, their nuisance value was considerable, with a few aircraft often causing sleepless nights over large areas of the country and regularly disrupting production at factories engaged in essential war work. In addition, they were also a valuable way for the bomber crews to learn the art of night navigation, but as the attackers immediately started to use the radio beams associated with the highly secret 'Knickebein' electronic bombing and navigation aid over British targets this system, the only one available to the whole bomber force, was soon compromised and successfully jammed.

Bristol, Bathurst Basin. (Floating Harbour), target GB 45 52. Document bc, the annotated photograph, taken at about 7.30am on the morning of 30 June 1940 by an aircraft from Aufklärungsgruppe Ob.d.L. and issued in March 1941.

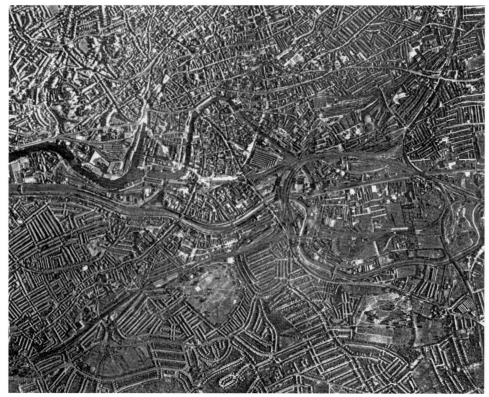

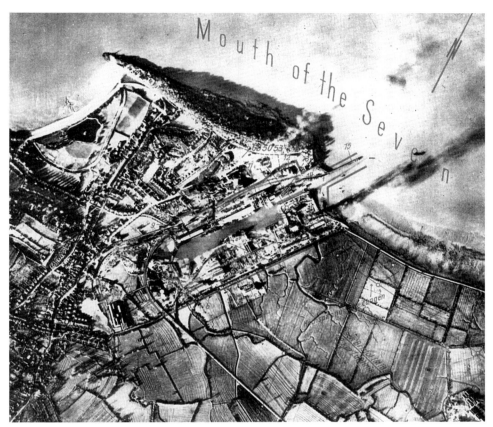

Portishead, harbour installations, target GB 45 56. Document bc, the annotated photograph, taken at about 3.15pm on the afternoon of 26 November 1940 by an aircraft from Aufklärungsgruppe Ob.d.L. and issued in April 1941.

In order to maintain the pressure on the defences, it had also been ordered that, in spite of the danger, during daylight hours surprise pinpoint attacks were to be undertaken against specific important targets, usually associated with the local docks or aircraft industry. These were to be carried out either by single or, at the most, small groups of aircraft, and although generally flown by crews specially selected for their skill and experience, it soon became necessary to permit them only when sufficient cloud cover was available, in order to give some degree of protection from interception by RAF fighters. By the late summer such missions had been christened 'Pirate' attacks by the Luftwaffe crews, and the first of these directed at a target in the Bristol area was the unsuccessful attempt on Portishead Docks by three Junkers 88s from II./KG 51 during the early evening of 3 July.

During the following afternoon a further raid was undertaken against the Bristol Aeroplane Company by a lone Heinkel from III./KG 54 carrying the identification code B3+DM on the side of its fuselage. Although to begin with the mission went reasonably well, with slight damage being

Part of the balloon barrage
protecting Bristol City Docks.
(Author's Collection)

The parachute delivered LMB 1,000kg sea mine. When fitted with an impact fuse this weapon was also employed against British cities, and in this country became known as the Land Mine. *(via G. Morley)*

caused to the roof of the firm's Rodney Works, after attacking the bomber was quickly intercepted by the three Spitfires from No.92 Squadron flown by Sergeant R.H. Fokes and Pilot Officers H.D Edwards and C.H. Saunders, all on daytime deployment at Filton. They quickly caught up with the enemy in the vicinity of Weston-super-Mare, and after a running fight across Somerset finally forced the raider down just over the border near Gillingham, in Dorset, the wireless operator being the only one of the four crew members to survive the action. Ironically this was also one of the last missions carried out by III./KG 54, as on 11 July it was withdrawn from operations and soon after disbanded, its place in Luftflotte 3's Order of Battle being taken by KGr 806, a Junkers 88 equipped coastal attack unit transferred from the navy.

As well as attacking important factories, the Germans also began tightening the blockade of the country, and following the closure of much of the east coast to British shipping aerial minelaying operations were extended to cover the important shipping lanes and harbour entrances on the western side of the country. Consequently, the Bristol Channel and Severn Estuary were visited for the first time by the Heinkel 111 minelayers of Dutch based I./KG 4 on the night of 17 July, and in order to maintain the pressure on the defences and to interrupt vital war production, these missions were usually flown on nights when no harassing attacks were taking place, thereby extending the amount of time people were forced to spend uncomfortably in air raid shelters. 1,000kg parachute mines released at low altitude were used to block the sea lanes, and it was fortunate that Germans were unaware of the fact that to begin with the defenders were totally unable to track minelaying aircraft operating over the Bristol Channel. As this almost deprived shipping of the use of Avonmouth Docks, to combat the new menace the Observer Corps network was extended to cover Devon and Cornwall, and further radar stations capable of detecting the low flying Heinkels were ordered to supplement the lone installation in Cornwall.

Strengthening the Western Flank

With the Luftwaffe now paying regular visits to the West Country constant improvements had to be made to the area's fighter defences, the most important of which saw the Filton, Pembrey, and St Eval Sectors becoming part of a new No.10 (Fighter) Group, which began work on 8 July. The establishment of this had in fact been contemplated before the war, and in February 1940 construction work had started on the new headquarters at Rudloe Manor in Box, near Bath. From here the Group was to oversee the defence of the whole of South West England and South Wales, something it was in a better position to carry out when on 3 August it finally took over responsibility for the Middle Wallop Sector, so important for protecting Bristol. When No.10 Group first went into action its commander had four squadrons to divide between his three Sectors, and for some months afterwards he continued to lack any purpose-built Sector headquarters, or sufficiently well-equipped aerodromes in suitable locations. Nevertheless, the situation was slowly improving and 5 July saw the Hurricanes of No.87 Squadron arrive at Exeter, while on the 11 they joined flights from No.92 Squadron in alternate weekly deployments at Hullavington, with both squadrons operating during the month from the aerodrome's Relief Landing Ground at Babdown Farm, near Tetbury in Gloucestershire. However, there remained many problems in carrying out operational night flying alongside flying training, and so in early August the fighters were transferred to a grass airfield at nearby Bibury.

Bristol's heavy anti-aircraft defences were also strengthened during July 1940, and by 10 July the manning was completed of eight semi-mobile 3" guns which had been installed on two new sites, one at Whitchurch and the other, named Reservoir, on Bedminster Down. An additional five heavy gun positions were also built during the next couple of months, although it was to be some time before the majority of them, located at Avonmouth, Almondsbury, Hambrook, Hanham and Henbury, received any weapons. By this time the deployment of the balloon barrages around the Bristol area was at last completed, and by the end of July some 32 balloons were flying at Avonmouth, 24 at Filton and 40 around central Bristol. More passive forms of defence had also been put into place during the first summer of war, and these included the camouflage of important buildings and the construction, by the Air Ministry, of dummy airfields for daytime use and realistic looking flarepaths designed to confuse enemy bomber crews at night, so luring them away from authentic aerodromes. Not only airfields were decoyed but other 'Key Points' such as aircraft factories and harbours also needed to be covered, so in August 1940 decoy sites incorporating lights and fires were introduced for night protection. In the Bristol area a decoy for the Filton works was established at Patchway, while others to designed to simulate the local port facilities were built at Long Ashton, Severn Beach, Lawrence Weston, and Portbury.

CHAPTER 3

THE EAGLE TIGHTENS ITS GRIP

August to October 1940

Since the fall of France Hitler had waited in vain for word from London that the Government was ready to negotiate an end to hostilities. Nevertheless, although he still firmly believed that the British people themselves really wanted peace, he ordered that the country should be bombed into submission, as threatening to carry out 'Unternehmen Seelöwe' ('Operation Sealion'), the invasion of England, would not be enough to cause a popular rising against the existing leadership, for in reality 'Sealion' was nothing more than a gigantic bluff! So, in order to keep up the psychological pressure on the British public, at the beginning of August, German bombers flew over various parts of the country dropping leaflets, upon which were printed extracts from Hitler's 'Last Appeal to Reason' speech of 19 July. The first such sorties were carried out on the night of 1 August when Bristol and Southampton were the targets for the four Heinkel 111s from II./KG 55 flying

from Chartres. However, due to a combination of bad navigation and poor visibility over the target area those intended for Bristol fell in Brecon, and at Backwell in Somerset. That night also saw the Parnall Aircraft plant at Yate targeted for the first time, but again neither of the two Heinkels from II./KG 55 succeeded in locating any of their objectives at Yate, Filton or Avonmouth.

As a prelude to the Luftwaffe's proposed bombardment of Britain, the all-important elimination of the RAF and its associated aircraft industry was scheduled to begin in early August, a process which it was hoped would take about a month, after which the onslaught could begin in earnest. The day for

A German poster proclaiming 'Unsere Luftwaffe' – 'Our Luftwaffe'. *(Author's Collection)*

its launching was given the code name of 'Adler Tag' ('Eagle Day'), and although provisionally fixed for 10 August, due to poor weather conditions was postponed until the afternoon of 13 August, when the full might of the Luftwaffe was at last unleashed against Britain. As this change of tactics called for I./KG 4 to join the regular bomber force in attacks on Eastern England, the two Luftmines laid off Avonmouth early on the morning of 13 August were the last to be deployed by this unit during a two-month campaign that had seen their mines sink two vessels in the Seven Estuary. Although by this time over 800 bombers were available to Luftflotte 2 for operations over Eastern England, to carry out attacks on the western side of the country only about 480 such aircraft were on the strength of Luftflotte 3, these comprising the Junkers 88s of KG 51, KG 54, LG 1 and KGr 806, as well as the Heinkel 111s operated by KG 27, KG 55 and the recently arrived KGr 100. This latter unit was a particularly useful addition to the Order of Battle as its aircraft were the only ones in the Luftwaffe equipped to operate with an advanced precision radio beam bombing aid known as X-Verfahren. In addition, this somewhat inadequate force received something of a boost towards the end of August with the transfer from the navy of KGr 606, a coastal attack formation which brought with them some 30 of so old Dornier 17s.

With the 'Eagle' offensive finally under way, on the afternoon of 14 August German bombers ranged far and wide over the West of England and Wales engaged in 'armed reconnaissance' against RAF airfields and aircraft factories, but unfortunately for the Luftwaffe, late in the day three Heinkel 111s from III./KG 27 were shot down in quick succession over the Severn Estuary by Spitfires of No.92 Squadron, with two of the raiders crashing to earth in Somerset. These, and other heavy losses suffered elsewhere that day, had far reaching consequences, forcing Luftflotte 3 to return to the night bombing of inland targets, which although inherently less accurate than sorties flown in daylight, was likely to result in the loss of very few aircraft. So it was that just before midnight on 15 August elements of II./KG 27 took-off to carry out nuisance attacks on objectives in South Wales and the West, one of which was the Bristol Aeroplane Company's premises upon which returning crews claimed their Heinkels had dropped some 40 50kg high explosives. Sadly, 13 of these fell in the residential part of Filton and resulted in the death in hospital of 14-year-old Mervyn Bradley and his 66-year-old grandmother, the first fatalities to be suffered in the district, while 16 other bombs caused some minor damage to the BAC's East Works and the nearby RAF aerodrome.

Owing to bad weather a period relative calm set in on 19 August, and this lasted until the evening of 22 August when conditions improved enough to allow KGr 100 to carry out their first precision attack under Luftflotte 3, the target chosen again being the Bristol Aeroplane Company. The operation against Filton involved 23 Heinkel 111s which were dispatched from KGr 100's newly established base at Vannes, in Brittany, the aircraft all flying along an approach beam radiated from a transmitter at Cherbourg. During this raid, which lasted from 23.19pm until 2.50am, nearly 17 tonnes of high explosives and 576 incendiaries were dropped, and for the first time in an attempt against a target in the Bristol area nearly every bomb fell relatively close to the objective. Although only four people were injured considerable damage was caused to the BAC works, in particular at No.4 Factory and No.11 Test Bed, while once again a lack of effective night defences ensured that all the participating German aircraft returned safely to base.

Filton, Aircraft Works of the Bristol Aeroplane Company Ltd., target GB 74 52. Document b, the photograph, taken about 4.40pm on 27 September 1940 by a Junkers 88 of 3.(F)/123 and issued in November 1940.

Down below on the ground the company's staff reacted quickly and while the bombs were still falling Frederick Rose, a maintenance engineer in charge of a salvage party, led his two assistants into one of the damaged buildings where, although hampered by flood water and darkness, he personally extinguished a number of fires which had started among stored magnesium. He then moved on to another affected area where he assisted in checking several more outbreaks of fire, his personal courage and coolness at all times providing an outstanding example to his men. In recognition of this, on 30 September 1940 he was awarded the George Medal, the first person in the Bristol area to receive such a decoration.

A Switch to the Western Ports

In an attempt to make the best use of the available bombers the following night, 23 August, Luftflotte 3 began to step up attacks on the next most important targets in Britain, the vital west coast ports

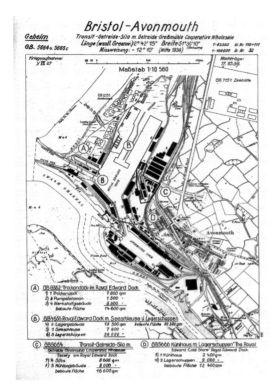

Bristol-Avonmouth

Geheim
GB. 5664 u. 5665c

Transit - Getreide - Silo m. Getreide - Großmühle Cooperative Wholesale
Länge (wesll.Greenw.)2°42'15' Breite51°30'10'
Maßweisung: - 12° 10' (Mitte 1938)

Bristol-Avonmouth, grain silos and large mill of the Co-Operative Wholesale Co., targets GB 56 64 and GB 56 65. Document c, the plan issued on 17 October 1938.

at Avonmouth and Liverpool. Locally, it was a clear night allowing Bristol's heavy guns to fire 156 rounds at the raiders, and although during a two hour period the crews of 31 Heinkel 111s from I., II. and III./KG 27 claimed to have dropped 21.7 tonnes of high explosives, 2.25 tonnes of oil bombs and 864 incendiaries on harbour facilities at Bristol and Avonmouth, the vast majority fell harmlessly over the east of the city and in parts of North Somerset, probably as a result of accurate gunfire. The next night all three gruppen of KG 27, returned to Bristol, but on this occasion also accompanied by the Junkers 88s of I. and III./LG 1, a total of 44 aircraft, the crews of which were again to briefed to bomb harbour installations in the Bristol area. The outward flight went fairly well and some 41 crews subsequently reported over the city, attacking with 27 tonnes of high explosive, 13 tonnes of oil bombs and 5,364 incendiaries in a raid which lasted over seven hours. The operation, however, was not a success for although the weather in the Bristol area was generally fine, low cloud impeded visibility, with the result that although a few high explosives hit the residential part of Avonmouth, the majority of the bombs once again came down fairly harmlessly in North Somerset.

Liverpool was then selected for the first really heavy raid of the war and on the night of 28 August 160 bombers set out with orders to destroy the city's harbour facilities, while the crews of a further 23 Dornier 17s of KGr 606 were briefed to make a diversionary attack on Bristol, where they subsequently claimed to have dropped nearly 10 tonnes of high explosives and 900 incendiaries. Locally the weather steadily deteriorated throughout the night, with heavy cloud varying in intensity with altitude, ensuring that the attack was a complete failure, the only bombs falling in the Bristol area being those reported at Lawrence Weston, Almondsbury, Olveston and Keynsham.

In spite of the determined efforts made by the RAF's fledgling night fighter force since the Luftwaffe had begun night raiding back in June, it was not until the night of 29 August, during another large scale attack on Liverpool, that they achieved their first confirmed local victory. This took place shortly before midnight when Flight Lieutenant A.R. Wright, flying a Spitfire of No.92 Squadron, operating out of Bibury, caught Heinkel 111 1G+EL of I./KG 27 illuminated in searchlight beams over Bristol, one of the six aircraft attempting to bomb the city as an alternative target. Wright immediately attacked the raider which eventually crashed near Fordingbridge, in Hampshire, after the crew had taken to their parachutes. This, however, was a unique triumph for No.10 Group's Spitfires as they were withdrawn from night operations soon after, their narrow undercarriage configuration having been responsible a number of night landing accidents. Nevertheless, the defence capability did not suffer too much, as during mid-August much needed gun laying radar at last started to be installed on heavy anti-aircraft sites around Bristol and this apparatus, with a range of about 23 miles, at last made possible reasonably good unseen fire control.

During the first week of September the bombers of Luftflotte 3 continued to attack Liverpool, with Bristol again being selected as a secondary target to divert the British defences. Accordingly, the Bristol City Docks, together with Avonmouth and Portishead, were bombed by 31 Junkers 88s and Heinkel 111s from I.,II. and III./KG 51 and I. and III./KG 55 on the night of 1 September, with 21 Heinkel 111s of Stab, I. and III./KG 55 returning on the night of 3 September to attack Bristol and Avonmouth, and 47 Junkers 88s and Heinkel 111s of, I., II., and III./KG 51, II./LG 1, I./KG 27, and I. and II./KG 55 reporting over the same targets the following night, in what was to be the last in this series of raids. The attacks on the west-coast harbours were the heaviest yet experienced in Britain and, although Luftwaffe casualties were minimal, no aircraft at all being lost against Bristol, the result were not particularly good, the bombing lacking the concentration required to cause any lasting disruption. However, during the period 22 August to 5 September a total of 25 people had been killed and 94 injured in Bristol and the surrounding area as a result of the 135 tonnes of high explosives, 39 tonnes of oil bombs, and 8,820 1kg incendiaries dropped by Luftwaffe bombers.

An unusual feature of the raids on Bristol during early September was the complete reliance upon oil bombs for fire raising, with a total of 105 of these weapons being dropped during the three nights. It was one of these devices which, at midnight on 1 September, was responsible for the tragic incident at Bigwoods, the fish merchants in Baldwin Street, where both the caretaker and her husband lost their lives as the bomb hit the building, burst into flames, and sprayed its contents through a window and over the nearby roadway, where wooden blocks were immediately set alight. Within seconds the whole of the top storey of the premises was also a mass of flames, and it was these that trapped May and Matthew Appleby in their bedroom, leaving neither of the poor souls with any way to escape from the raging inferno. Horrific though this was, by a miracle a

This unexploded SC 1800 'Satan' bomb fell at Beckington Road, Knowle, during the raid on the night of 3 January 1941. It was not recovered until 14 April 1943 and subsequently had a place of honour in the London Victory Parade. *(BUP)*

female relative who shared the accommodation with them was successfully rescued and rushed off to hospital, albeit suffering from burns to various parts of her body.

In spite of the fact that the relatively small-scale attacks carried out against the Bristol area between mid-June and early September 1940 had inflicted little serious damage, they had assisted the local defences in perfecting their organisation under combat conditions, and this was especially true of the Royal Engineers bomb disposal units. A good example was the successful defusing of 250kg bombs at Congresbury, in Somerset, on 17 August and at Temple Street, Bristol, on 3 September, by Lieutenant Edward Womersley Reynolds of No.102 Bomb Disposal Section, whose bravery in making safe weapons on which he had not been trained was rewarded on 17 September 1940 with the award of the Empire Gallantry Medal, which seven days later was automatically replaced by the newly introduced George Medal.

The Battle of the Factories

Over on the Eastern side of the country, on the night of 24 August, German bombers had accidentally dropped bombs on Central London and this, seen by the British as an escalation of the air war, resulted in the War Cabinet sanctioning the first raid against Berlin, which was carried out the following night. Yet again Hitler was enraged, and as a result London superseded Fighter Command as the primary target of the Luftwaffe. Reichsmarschall Hermann Göring, the Luftwaffe's commander in chief, assumed direct command of the air offensive against Britain on 7 September, and that afternoon the Luftwaffe flew its first large-scale raid against London. The bombers returned that night, and this marked the beginning of a series of raids that was to last for 65 days, causing many of Luftflotte 3's aircraft previously available to carry out attacks on the Bristol area being ordered to temporarily re-direct their efforts to the capital.

Early September also saw the temporary transfer to Luftflotte 3 of 86 Messerschmitt 110s, a force made up of 26 fighter-bombers from Epr Gr 210, and 86 long-range fighters from ZG 26, with

The Messerschmitt Bf 110C long-range fighter. This type was also used as a fighter-bomber. *(via G. Morley)*

which it was hoped to be able to carry out a series of systematic daylight pinpoint attacks on some of the most important British aircraft factories. At the same time it was ordered that if the weather situation prevented large-scale operations against London, then surprise daylight 'Pirate' attacks by individual bomber aircraft were also to be made on targets associated with the British aircraft industry. These were to be flown in low cloud and often appalling conditions in an attempt to prevent interception by RAF fighters, and the first such operation carried out against a target in the Bristol area was the unsuccessful attempt, by a lone Heinkel from I./KG 55, to bomb the Bristol Aeroplane Company at Filton on 16 September.

As the invasion bluff had now run its full course and the bombing campaign still had not succeeded in forcing Britain to the negotiating table, on 19 September instructions were issued to step up the attacks against the all important British aircraft industry, both by night and day, by reducing the size of the formations engaged in raids on London. Accordingly the bomber force of Luftflotte 3 was once again assigned the most important targets on the western side of Britain, and as part of a new strategy 25 September saw the start of a planned series of large-scale daylight attacks on the aircraft industry in the West Country, during which cover to and from the objective was to be provided by the recently arrived long-range fighters. The target that morning was again the Bristol Aeroplane Company's plant, and on this occasion Luftflotte 3 ordered 68 Heinkel 111s of Stab, I., II. and III./KG 55, escorted by 52 Messerschmitt 110s of I.,II. and III./ZG 26, to undertake the operation, this aerial armada coming in over Portland at 11.23am before flying across country to Weston-super-Mare where they turned right and started the run-in to their objective. However, as Fighter Command assumed that the Westland works at Yeovil was the destination for the raiders they suffered only an inconclusive engagement with the Spitfires of No.152 Squadron from Warmwell before they arrived over North Somerset. Here, minutes out from the target, Heinkel G1+DN of II./KG 55 was fired upon by men of 237 Battery, 76th HAA Regiment at the Portishead gunsite and hit by their initial salvo, forcing the five-man crew to bale out of the aircraft which eventually spiralled down into a field at Failand, the first of only two enemy aircraft to be destroyed by the city's anti-aircraft guns during World War Two. Locally the weather was perfect for bombing, with banks of thick cloud broken by patches of clear blue sky, and the rest of the formation took full advantage of it, 58 Heinkels attacking the BAC works at about 11.45am with 81.5 tonnes of high explosives and six tonnes of oil bombs, all of which fell on the factory and surrounding districts in just 45 seconds.

As a result of subsequent de-briefings and photographs taken during the attack and by a reconnaissance sortie flown over Filton later that day, the Germans knew that the raid had been a great success, even though KG 55 had lost four

Heinkel He 111s of Kampfgeschwader 55 en-route for Filton on the morning of 25 September 1940. *(via G. Morley)*

The Bristol Beaufighter 1F. *(BAC)*

Henikels and ZG 26 three Messerschmitts. Accordingly the Luftwaffe's own magazine, *Der Adler*, soon after proudly proclaimed: 'This factory will not produce many more aircraft', while Major Friedrich Kless, the attack leader and Gruppenkommandeur of II./KG 55, was awarded the Ritterkruz on 14 October. The Luftwaffe certainly had good cause to celebrate as eight newly built aircraft, including two precious prototypes of the Bristol Beaufighter, the new and desperately needed night interceptor, had been destroyed and production at the plant temporarily halted. Serious damage had been caused at the Rodney Works, while there and at the Flight Shed and East Engine Works direct hits were made on a number of workers shelters, tragic incidents which did much to account for the fact that of the 132 people killed, 91 were BAC employees, while another 315 sustained various degrees of injury, in and around the plant.

Immediately after the bombs had stopped falling Mr E.W. King, a works foreman, dealt with a number of fire calls and afterwards went to help at the partly underground shelters, six of which had received direct hits, and here he found that some were just indentations in the ground, their roofs having completely collapsed on the occupants, while others had burst wide open exposing their contents to the sky. Some shelters contained dismembered bodies and although in many cases the clothing had been burned off the side that had exposed to the explosion, the other side was intact. As if this was not bad enough, elsewhere it was discovered that the corpses were rammed up against one end of the shelter, as if they had been pushed there by a giant piston. During the course of the day Mr King and two assistants were forced to pick up the remains with their hands as there was no other way to do the job, and many times a head or a limb came away separately, while one individual's head had a large round hole right down through from the top, with nothing inside. When the gruesome work had been completed the three men laid everything on the floor of two lorries,

The remains of Heinkel He 111, G1+DN of 5./KG 55, shot down by AA fire at Racecourse Farm, Failand, on 25 September. *(Jim Facey)*

and after a tarpaulin had been found to cover the pitiful remains they were driven to the temporary mortuary set up in St Peter's Church Hall opposite the BAC headquarters building.

Included in the bomb load carried by I./KG 55 were 17 delayed action 250kg bombs which in the hours following the raid were to cause serious difficulties for the emergency services. Nevertheless, Clifford Bruce Dunning, a Bristol ARP Plotting Officer, immediately volunteered to report on these and was examining one of the devices when another that he had checked only a few minutes before suddenly exploded. Luckily he was far enough away to escape injury, though fragments of the exploding bomb and pieces of debris flew all around him. Undeterred by this experience, Dunning continued to visit and report on a large number of unexploded bombs, both then and during later attacks, and for the courage he displayed in undertaking such highly dangerous work, and in particular for his efforts at Filton, on 14 March 1941, he was awarded the George Cross.

For the local defences it had been a bad day, for not only had the majority of the raiders reached and successfully bombed the BAC plant, they had also scored direct hits on a barrage balloon site at Filton manned by No.935 Squadron and one of 354 Battery's searchlight sites at Stoke Gifford, killing an operator at each location. The initial confusion as to the German's ultimate target ensured that none of the enemy were brought down by the main force of Hurricanes and Spitfires until after the attack had taken place, and although a total of seven German aircraft were subsequently destroyed for the loss of just one RAF pilot, the damage caused at Filton did emphasise the importance of having a fighter squadron permanently stationed in the immediate vicinity of Bristol, none having been so deployed since April. Fortunately, as it was to turn out, Fighter Command acted swiftly and the very next day the Hurricane equipped No.504 Squadron was transferred from

Hendon to Filton while, in order to supplement the heavy anti-aircraft gun ring around the factories, on 27 September eight 3" semi-mobile guns were moved from the Whitchurch and Reservoir sites to Henbury and Almondsbury.

The arrival of the Hurricanes proved most providential as on the morning of Friday 27 September German aircraft in reappeared in daylight over Bristol when 10 Messerschmitt 110 fighter/bombers from Epr Gr 210, escorted by 42 of the long-range fighter version belonging to I.,II. and III./ZG 26, attempted a pinpoint attack on the Parnall Aircraft works at Yate. Over the West Country the weather was fair, with patches of cloud, and for the citizens of Bristol this offered the unique opportunity to witness a classic 'dog-fight' over the city as the newly arrived fighters completely routed the raiders, forcing them to jettison their bombs in the vicinity of Filton and run for home. During this action two escorting Messerschmitts of I./ZG 26 were shot down by No.504 Squadron with one of these, U8+GL, the victim of Sergeant H.D.B. Jones, crashing on to a hillside at Haydon, near Radstock, after being abandoned by its crew, while the other, U8+FK, disintegrated over the Stapleton Institution at Fishponds following an engagement with Flying Officer Michael Royce. From the wreckage of this, the only enemy aircraft to fall inside the Bristol boundary during World War Two, were recovered the bodies of Oberleutnant Hans Tiepelt, the pilot, and Unteroffizier Herbert Brosig, the wireless operator/air gunner, and both were subsequently laid to rest with full military honours in nearby Greenbank Cemetery.

The remains of the crew of Messerschmitt Bf 110, U8+FK of 2./ZG 26, shot down over the Stapleton Institution, Fishponds, on 27 September. *(Jim Facey)*

Greenbank Cemetery. The graves of Oberfeldwebel Hans Tiepelt and Unteroffizier Herbert Brosig who were killed when their Messerschmitt Bf 110 crashed at Fishponds on 27 September 1940. *(Author's Collection)*

Upon his return to Filton, Royce composed a brief combat report which revealed that when his squadron attacked the Messerschmitt escorts they were approaching Filton at 12,000ft, a fact which helped give rise to the rumour that the BAC had again been the target. He continued by saying that;

'They broke formation and started climbing, but I got on to one and fired a burst of three seconds. White smoke came from its port engine. I then noticed an enemy aircraft on my tail and did a steep turn to get onto its tail. I then fired a long burst of nearly 10 seconds, and white smoke came from both its engines. The enemy aircraft then dived into the yard of a house in East Bristol, exploded and burst into flames.'

During this ill-fated attempt on Yate Epr Gr 210 lost a number of irreplaceable senior officers including their Gruppenkommandeur, Hauptmann Martin Lutz, and before the day had ended a total of four Messerschmitts from Epr Gr 210 and six from ZG 26 had been destroyed. The Luftwaffe obviously could not sustain such an attrition rate, and thus was brought to a premature end this type of daylight operation by fighter-bombers against targets in the West Country. Nevertheless, large-scale daylight attacks using conventional bombers continued to be undertaken into October, but following an attempt against the Westland aircraft factory at Yeovil which resulted in nine aircraft being shot down, seven of them Messerschmitt long-range fighters, Göring was happy to use the onset of poor weather as an excuse to call-off these costly operations.

Monitoring Bristol's Morale

As the bombing of Britain intensified during the late summer and autumn of 1940 it became ever more important for the government to be in a position to accurately gauge the morale of the civilian population, and in order to accomplish this the Ministry of Home Security's Home Intelligence Unit were charged with producing regular reports. Also involved in this work was Mass Observation, a social survey organisation set up in 1937 to keep its fingers on the pulse of the nation, its specially selected volunteers being instructed to keep diaries in which to record the population's reaction to the ever-changing wartime conditions. This they achieved by the simple expedient of eavesdropping on people's conversations in such public places as pubs, shops and cinemas, and as the morale in the larger towns and cities was of particular interest, several such observers were active in Bristol

The wreckage of Messerschmitt Bf 110, U8+FK of 2./ZG 26, in front of the nurses home at the Stapleton Institution, Fishponds. *(BUP)*

The Stapleton Institution in Manor Road, Fishponds, later became Blackberry Hill Hospital, but has now been closed and awaits redevelopment.

throughout the war. Their work was also supplemented by the organisation's special investigation team which was sent into 'blitzed' cities shortly after large-scale attacks, and in the case of Bristol these visits were to be undertaken in December 1940 and during March and April 1941.

At the end of August 1940 observers had already come to the conclusion that Bristolians believed that any enemy aircraft flying over the area, with or without hostile intent, was actually an air raid. Although this did mean that the population quickly became used to living under the threat of attack, the very small amount of bombing actually encountered lead many of them, including some of the city's more prominent citizens, to seriously underestimate the value of the special protective measures that had been put in place. Although this attitude was not unique to Bristol, locally it was particularly noticeable as during most raids the public shelters remained practically empty, only the Filton attack of 25 September being heavy enough to force the closure of some of the city's shops. This, the area's first taste of things to come, also left many BAC workers with little faith in the factory's own shelters, with the result that for many months after there was a mass exodus of staff whenever the siren sounded, the 'Filton Harriers', as they became known, making a dash to either the local golf course or to the safety of a nearby railway tunnel.

Pirates Ahoy!

Throughout October London continued to be the principal target for the long-range bombers, it being raided every night. However, with the blockade of Britain being tightened the Luftwaffe High Command was able to order more bombing effort to be put into night harassing attacks on the harbour installations at Bristol, Liverpool and Glasgow, with the industrial centres of Birmingham and Coventry as alternative targets, while still maintaining the pressure on the capital. As a result, four whole bomber Geschwader were transferred from Luftflotte 2 to Luftflotte 3, immediately adding to the latter's inventory the Heinkel 111s belonging to I./KG 1 and the whole of KG 26, as well as the Junkers 88s from II./KG 76 and all three gruppen of KG 77. However, the other elements of KG 1 and KG 76 were either engaged in, or about to undergo, conversion to the Junkers, a process that was not finally completed until April 1941.

Silhouette of the Junkers Ju 88. *(Author's Collection)*

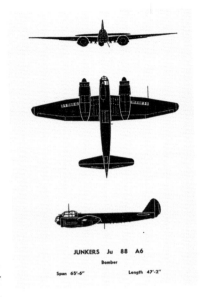

JUNKERS Ju 88 A6
Bomber
Span 65'-6"   Length 47'-2"

During October, Luftflotte 3 was also ordered to step-up pin-point 'Pirate' daylight attacks by single aircraft against important centres of the British aircraft industry when weather permitted, and so the plants at Filton and Yate once again became prime targets. Operations commenced on 6 October when a lone Heinkel from II./KG 55 attempted an afternoon raid on Yate, but the Parnall plant remained untouched as before the attack could be carried out the essential cloud cover started to break up, forcing the crew to bomb Bournemouth as an alternative. These missions were also interspersed with more conventional operations by single night bombers, with Filton being targeted twice, and Yate once in unsuccessful attacks carried out by II. and III./KG 55 between 10 and 15 October. With the return of suitable weather conditions the daytime 'Pirate' attacks resumed on 15 October, when Oberleutnant Johannes Speck von Sternburg, the Staffelkapitän of 9 Staffel, KG 55, made an abortive attempt against Filton, which was followed by three more unsuccessful sorties later in the month by the same crew. On 19 October the mission was again aborted, on 24 October the bombs fell at Yatton, while on 31 October the Royal Ordnance Factory at Glascoed in South Wales was bombed after being mistaken for Filton, an attack for which the crew received a mention in the 'High Command of the Armed Forces Communiqué' issued on 2 November.

The autumn also saw the minelaying unit KGr 126 transfer its Heinkel 111s to Brittany and assume full responsibility for sowing aerial mines around the British coast, from the Isle of Wight to the Irish Sea. As it had been some months since minelayers had operated in the Bristol Channel and Severn Estuary, in order to tighten the blockade of Britain on 12 October the Luftwaffe High Command issued new instruction for the prosecution of the air war against Britain's western flank, and these included the mining of the vital shipping lanes off Avonmouth.

As a result of this directive KGr 126 made their first appearance over the Bristol Channel on the evening of 24 October and between then and 22 December, when the formation was re-designated I./KG 28, they were responsible for sinking four vessels and causing damage to another two in the Severn Estuary alone.

HE'S SAILING TOMORROW FOR...
SHE TALKED
...THIS HAPPENED
CARELESS TALK COSTS LIVES

CHAPTER 4

THE ONSLAUGHT BEGINS

November 1940

Although since early September the Luftwaffe had been battering London night after night in an attempt to force a British surrender, this policy was not proving at all successful as the bombing was too scattered over the great area of the metropolis to produce any large-scale destruction or collapse of civilian morale. Consequently, it was decided to change tactics by directing the night attacks more against Britain's manufacturing base, followed by a concentrated assault on the ports as part of the overall policy of blockade. While conducting these operations the

Bristol-South, Electric Light Works on the Feeder Canal, target GB 50 52. Document bc, the annotated photograph, taken at about 7.30am on the morning of 30 June 1940 by an aircraft from Aufklärungsgruppe Ob.d.L. and issued in August 1940.

Germans considered that any lack of training in night navigation and bomb aiming would be more than compensated by the use of their radio bombing beams, but as Knickebein was already suffering from jamming the Luftwaffe had to rely heavily upon two specialist units serving as pathfinders for the main bomber force, these being KGr 100 equipped with X-Verfahren and III./KG 26 operating the new and highly sophisticated Y-Verfahen electronic bombing aid. The main task of these pathfinders was to start fires during the early stages of an attack, the glow from which it was hoped would guide the main bomber force accurately to the target area, and it was unfortunate for the inhabitants of Bristol that countermeasures against both X and Y-Yerfahren were to prove relatively ineffective, allowing the Luftwaffe to operate largely unhindered at night throughout the winter of 1940–41.

The pathfinders were also assisted by II./KG 55, which although not equipped with electronic aids, acted as 'Illuminators', as they were particularly adept at finding their objectives at night. It was this unit that dropped not only parachute marker flares at the commencement of most major attacks, but also very high calibre bombs which it was hoped would smash the water mains in the target area and so hamper the fire-fighters. In addition, as the fledgling British night defences had so far proved to be almost totally ineffective against the Luftwaffe's bombers, it was decided that there was no need for the raids to be concentrated in time, so that whenever weather conditions permitted the attacks were made to last as long as possible, so as to cause maximum disruption to the war effort.

Initial instructions were issued on 8 November ordering preparations to be made for large scale attacks on manufacturing centres in the Midlands, the first of these taking place on the night of 14 November when widespread devastation was caused at Coventry. In Britain this raid highlighted the urgent need to attract enemy bombs away from targeted towns and cities, not only to protect the civil population and industry but also to keep up morale, and later in the month it led to the introduction of 'Special Fires', the idea being to disguise the effect of radio counter-measures activity by igniting specially built installations in what might appear to the enemy as his target area. To cover this plan, on 10 December the 'Special Fires' were code named 'Starfish' and a number of such sites were constructed locally, the first serving Bristol being laid out at Stockwood and Chew Magna. Additional installations were authorised soon after to provide further protection for the city, and these were subsequently set up at Downside near Brockley Combe, Kenn Moor, on Black Down near Cheddar, and Yeomouth near Kingston Seymour.

Terror and Death in the Streets of Bristol

Between 15 and 23 November German night bombers kept up the pressure on British cities, operating twice over London, three times over Birmingham and twice over Southampton, while on 24 November Bristol was selected for its first major attack, the purpose of which was to eliminate it as an "importing port supplying much of the Midlands and South of England". To accomplish this the crews of 148 bombers were briefed to attack, the 94 Heinkels, 49 Junkers and 5 Dorniers being drawn from KG 1, III./KG 26, II. and III./KG 27, I.,II. and III./KG 51, Stab,I.,II. and III./KG 55, KGr 100, KGr 606, and LG 1. The concentration point for the raiders was centred on the harbour and industrial plants on both sides of the City Docks, and to guide the pathfinders both

Wine Street from under the balcony of the Dutch House at the corner of High Street following the raid of 24 November. *(Jim Facey)*

Wine Street looking towards Broad Weir during the 1990s. *(Author's Collection)*

A view up Mary-le-Port Street from High Street following the raid of 24 November. The footbridge joined the retail part of Baker-Bakers premises in Wine Street with their wholesale department in Bridge Street. *(Jim Facey)*

X and Y-Verfahren beams were laid over Bristol, while to assist the rest of the attack force the Cherbourg, Morlaix and Dieppe Knickebein transmitters were also operating that evening.

The wind in the target area was moderate to gentle west-south-west, and although parachute flares were dropped by II./KG 55 at the commencement of the raid, and III./KG 26 attacked using Y-Verfahren, the crews from KGr 100 subsequently claimed to have employed only Dead Reckoning and Knickebein, in spite of the fact that the X-Beams were being radiated. Because of broken high cloud bombing was initially undertaken mostly by radio and 'Dead Reckoning' methods, but as the attack progressed the sky cleared and it became possible to bomb visually, guided by the fires which could be seen from over 150 miles away. To begin with, the run-up to target was from south to north, but later in the evening large cumulus clouds developed over the city as a result of the numerous fires, and some raiders were then tracked flying round Bristol and approaching from the north.

Typical of the attackers was Obleutnant Speck von Sternberg, from III./KG 55 who, together with his four other crew members, climbed aboard their Heinkel as dusk fell that evening. Loaded with sixteen 50kg high explosives and twelve BSK 36 incendiary bomb containers, the heavily-laden bomber finally took off at 6.44pm, and after making a turn, climbed slowly to an altitude of 20,000ft. The red afterglow of the setting sun was still lighting the western horizon as the Heinkel passed overhead radio beacon Willi at Cherbourg, from where course was set for a point in mid-Channel to intercept the Brest Knickebein beam that was to lead them on to Bristol. All went according to plan, and at 7.15pm the English coast was crossed to the accompaniment of lively but ineffective searchlight activity and anti-aircraft fire, while shortly afterwards, with their objective more than 50 miles distant, a huge fireglow came into sight indicating that the 'firelighters' had done their job well.

The weather over Dorset and Wiltshire was fine, and as he approached the target Feldwebel Martin Reiser, the navigator/bomb aimer, found the sight of Bristol on fire quite breathtaking, writing soon after that: 'Searchlights swept the sky above the already devastated city, where scattered clouds were reddened by a massive sea of fire, incessantly sprinkled with exploding high explosive bombs'. Over and on the approaches to Bristol the twinkling bursts of anti-aircraft shells added to the awesome sight with a spectacular but totally ineffective display. So, with little to fear, after descending to 14,800ft Reiser commenced his bombing run at 7.45pm, and had soon added to the conflagration below. On the return flight the crew could still see the fires raging in the stricken city from the south coast, and after routing via the radio beacons at Fécamp and Dreux, they eventually landed back at Villacoublay at 10.00pm, after which debriefing was followed by a meal and a good night's sleep.

For the Germans it had been a very successful night, the crews of some 135 aircraft having reported over Bristol between 6.30 and 11pm, claiming to have dropped 156.25 tonnes of high explosives, 4.75 tonnes of oil bombs and 12,500 incendiaries for the loss of just two bombers, a Heinkel from II./KG 55 shot down off Portsmouth by anti-aircraft fire, and a Dornier from KGr 606 which crashed near Plymouth after colliding with a nearby barrage balloon cable. Upon the return of the others the general impression gained from the participating airmen was that results were similar to those achieved at Birmingham and Coventry, causing the Germans to announce that

Wine Street looking from the top
of Union Street following the raid
of 24 November. *(Jim Facey)*

Looking down Park Street, with Charlotte Street off to the right, following the raid of 24 November.
(Jim Facey)

as a distributing centre and important railway junction Bristol had been wiped out. 'Of all the ports on the West Coast, Bristol' they said 'was the nearest and best situated for the Midlands, London and the South Coast!'

In stark contrast, and in spite of firing a total of 3,404 rounds at the raiders, the city's heavy anti-aircraft guns seemed powerless against the German onslaught, while a Hurricane of No.87 Squadron which inconclusively engaged an Heinkel 111 illuminated in a searchlight beam over Bristol was the best the locally based fighters could manage. Likewise, the balloons in the Bristol barrage fared badly, some fifteen either being set adrift or brought down with damage caused by bomb splinters, while an operator was also killed by a high explosive bomb which scored a direct hit on one of No.951 Squadron's balloon

Looking down Park Street in the 1990s. *(Author's Collection)*

sites. Bomb disposal experts were also kept busy with some 175 unexploded devices being left to be dealt with by the recently re-trained No.853 (Quarrying) Company RE which was to have sole responsibility for bomb disposal in the Bristol area for the following few months!

Not surprisingly the city was badly mauled, with the bombing resulting in the death of 200 Bristolians and injuries to a further 890, while up until the time the 'All Clear' finally sounded just after midnight some 307 incidents had been logged by ARP Control. Within a few hours of the attack starting much of the central shopping had become a massive conflagration, resulting in most of Castle Street, Wine Street and High Street being gutted by fire, along with parts of Clifton, where both the University Great Hall and the Princes Theatre were burnt out. There was also serious damage in the Knowle, Temple, Barton Hill and Eastville districts, while other large fires developed in St Philips' and around St James' Barton. The situation was probably made worse because the Fire Guard organisation had yet to be formed, and it being a Sunday evening the city centre was deserted with the majority of the commercial premises securely locked. To add to the problems, at this period most buildings lacked any easy access to their vulnerable roof areas where a single incendiary bomb could start a fire almost invisible to observers on the ground, and it was in this manner that a number of landmark buildings were lost.

Nevertheless, Bristol's Auxiliary Fire Service got off to a very good start, and within half an hour of the warning some 897 part-time AFS personnel had reported for duty, seven of whom subsequently

High Street looking from Christchurch tower towards George's Brewery following the raid of 24 November. *(Jim Facey)*

The site of the Dutch House at the corner of High Street and Wine Street during the 1990s. *(Author's Collection)*

lost their lives. In total 194 calls of fire were received, and as this completely overwhelmed the 224 available pumping appliances, at 7.38pm reinforcements were requested, this resulting in some 81 brigades arriving in the city from Gloucestershire, Somerset, Wiltshire, Hampshire, Dorset, Oxfordshire, Berkshire, Buckinghamshire, Surrey, London, Kent and South Wales, while 20,000ft of hose was also obtained from Cardiff, Newport, Bournemouth and Plymouth. To compound

The remains of Barton Warehouses at the corner of Barr's Street and St James's Barton following the raid of 24 November. *(Jim Facey)*

The burnt-out remains of the Dutch House at the corner of High Street and Wine Street following the raid of 24 November. *(Jim Facey)*

Taken from the roof of the Odeon cinema, this was the scene looking up Union Street towards Wine Street following the raid of 24 November. *(Jim Facey)*

the misery at 11.10pm the main water supply failed completely owing to damaged trunk mains, and water subsequently had to be obtained from the Floating Harbour, River Frome, and other supplementary supplies through direct and relay pumping. Operations continued throughout the night, and although shortly after daybreak the fires had been brought under control 26 were still smouldering and being attended to some 36 hours later.

ARP Wardens and Fire Watchers, both men and women, also battled with the thousands of incendiaries dropped by the raiders, and a number made the supreme sacrifice, the attack resulting in the death of a Fire Watcher, as well as 19 men, three women and two messengers from the Warden's Service. Many ordinary citizens were also trapped in wrecked buildings and Rescue Parties were called to 86 occurrences from which 137 persons were subsequently rescued alive and 107 bodies recovered. In spite of the falling bombs the medical, hospital and nursing staffs and those in charge of first-aid posts still managed to render speedy and efficient aid to the injured, although two ambulance drivers were killed while carrying out their work. Fortunately, the casualties, though heavy, were far below the number anticipated, and this was largely due to the centre of the city being less frequented on a Sunday than on business days. This having been said, large-scale disruption was caused to peoples lives and in the following 12 days the voluntary workers at Bristol's emergency hostels served some 70,294 meals to those deprived of cooking facilities or rendered homeless.

A Local Reporter's Scoop

Without doubt the most impressive and objective account of the raid was that written by Eric Buston, a reporter for the *Western Daily Press* which, although it was the scoop of his career, was not passed by the censor and so could not be made public until 1946.

'I was in Trinity Church, Whiteladies Road when last night's raid began. And if I preface my story of the more spectacular side of that unforgettable Sunday evening with an account of the more or less personal incidents in which I was concerned, it is because they glowed with the spirit of that will be worth remembering long after a new and greater Bristol has risen Phoenix-like from the ashes of the old. In a less deadly drama it would have been amusing. By about a quarter to seven it was obvious from the noise that this was not the mild an innocuous air raid to which we had become accustomed in recent months. Nevertheless, loud and ominous as were the bangs, the minister stuck resolutely to his original comfort that "they" were "only the friendly sound of guns", and with self-discipline which I fancy he learnt in the front line of the previous war, continued his extempore address with ordered precision right to the end. A long whiz and a splattering of metal more than once tested his voice, but "that is only shrapnel, I feel quite sure" he said cheerfully.'

'We opened the church doors and half Bristol seemed to be on fire! At that the congregation descended to the shelter of the underground schoolrooms. The air rang with

Narrow Wine Street following the raid of 24 November. *(Jim Facey)*

Stokes Croft looking from North Street following the raid of 24 November. The remains are those of Mickleburgh's piano store. *(Jim Facey)*

zooming planes and the barrage of the guns; the roof sang with the falling shrapnel. Now and then a thud told us of a high explosive bomb. You could read by the light of the fires – the nearest one a church [St Anselm's] not 50 yards away. Obviously, the schoolroom was indicated! With Coventry in mind, everyone prepared for a long night. The young people joked and knitted, the older ones talked (as they always will) and the children sat quiet and unsmiling by their parents knees. For some reason nobody suggested singing. I think it was such an obvious course that no one liked to broach it.'

'During the occasional lulls in the devil's symphony outside, odd groups slipped home. Others, from the half shelter of a surface archway, alternatively watched the show and ducked at the warning whistle of bombs and incendiaries. The roof of the burning church fell in, a house across the road caught fire, and southwards over Bristol the flames roared their fury to the sky. About half way through the raid (as it transpired) I got home, telephoned my unit, and found I was likely to be needed. My pass expired at 10.30 any way. So I borrowed my sister's bike and set off to return to camp [at Keynsham] and see what I could of the damage. It took me 25 minutes to reach the "Press" office in Baldwin Street, I remember I used to do it in five minutes years ago. I struck Whiteladies Road just above Clifton Down Station, and from there to the Centre, what with hosepipes and fires and endless detours, I pushed and carried that cycle as much as I rode it. On either side of my route, most of the streets had a house or two on fire, but they were nothing. With one or two exceptions I have reported every big fire in Bristol in the last ten years, but last night I saw twenty or so fires each one fiercer than I had seen before. Near the Whiteladies Cinema, Weeks' auction rooms and part of their furniture depository were one high storied mass of concentrated fire. Not so much flames as the red hot glow, magnified a thousand times, of a well fanned brazier. A hundred yards to the east St Joseph's Home in Cotham Hill was paying the price of a regime which knows not charity. Somewhere in Clifton, too, the flames had their hold, [Clifton Parish Church].'

'Down to the Victoria Rooms the road was clear, but there I should have stopped in amazement even had not the snaking hosepipe outside the Academy barred my path. Lennard's fine building (and the block including the Triangle behind) was one surging mass of fire. Firemen – professional and AFS, as everywhere, were valiant in heart and hands. But what could they do? I'll tell you what they did, though. They stopped that wave from flooding to the buildings neighbouring the Pro-Cathedral, and they stopped them from lapping and engulfing the eastern end of Queen's Road. For there was a nasty wind, and a mere 50ft of street would never have stemmed that tide. When, baulking at the fiery gauntlet of Queen's Road, I turned past the Embassy Cinema and went behind along Elmdale Road,

The burnt out shell of St Nicholas Church at the corner of High Street and Nicholas Street following the raid of 24 November. *(Jim Facey)*

Looking down High Street towards the
corner of St Nicholas Street during the
1990s. *(Author's Collection)*

the sparks from Lennards were falling
even there like fiendish snow. Up
Elton Road the handsome prep wing
of the Grammar School was burning
down.'

'I intended to turn down
University Road to join the main
street again, but a policeman said
"No", for the Art Gallery, that strange incongruous copy of the Doge's Palace in hostile
Venice, was well afire. Sharp cracks and crashes told of havoc among those treasured show
cases, and I feared [unnecessarily] for that fine new hall of the newer part of the Art Gallery.
I turned up University Road again towards the Royal Fort – and on my right the University
was ablaze. Obviously the fire went deep into the heart of the place, but I didn't realise, as

The Upper Arcade looking from the Horsefair towards St James's Barton following the raid of 24
November. The gentleman sketching among the ruins is Gordon Hake, the principal of the School of
Architecture. *(Jim Facey)*

I actually rode down Woodland Road, that the Great Hall was gone. Enough for me that the great Gothic tower still stood defiant to the blood-shot sky.'

'Somehow, the Prince's Theatre in Park Row gave me a nasty shock, because, although I've always grumbled at its design, it stood for so many peace-time things that I love – the D'Oyly Carte, the ballet, good plays and cheerful music. No Prince's panto this year. By this time the shrapnel from the guns, the occasional explosions and the odd planes still overhead just failed to register in my consciousness. I had to get back to camp; but, after all, I am a journalist, and one day (censor permitting!) this story would have to be written. So I turned right at the bottom of Woodland Road, intent on going down Park Street. I nearly regretted that impulse. Boot's was ablaze in Queen's Road, but I hardly noticed it. My eyes fell down the hills to the city. Park Street was ablaze, it seemed, from end to end. It was an avenue of fire. Because of its proportions I suppose, the effect was exaggerated, because when I returned a day or two later I was surprised to see the destruction was not greater. But to me on that night of amazement, Park Street was the most shocking sight of all. The road was covered with glass and stones and steel and hosepipes. Fire engines steadily roared their applause to the heroic effort of the firemen fighting impossible odds. I carried my cycle down through an avenue of flame which seemed to be straining to join its hungry hands across the cringing thoroughfare. The heat was considerable, and I veered from one side to

Bristol Bridge looking towards the corner of Victoria Street following the raid of 24 November. *(Jim Facey)*

the other, according to the intensity of the flanking fires, to avoid its worst. As before, I was glad of my eyeshields and tin hat because of the sparks and the nerve-jumping crashes of falling masonry.'

'When I got to the bottom of Park Street and looked back at this mighty torch flaming to the skies, I estimated that every third shop was ablaze. Stopping to test my tyres, I reflected, perhaps a trifle sardonically, that there could be few people in Bristol who would not derive pleasure from the fact that so far, at least, the Cathedral, the new civic buildings and the *Mauritania* were unscathed! Along the alleyway by the Lord Mayor's Chapel a glow told of further mischief afloat. At the end of College Green, Gane's furniture shop was burning like tinder, but round the corner – surprise and relief – the Centre was its accustomed Sunday self – except that it was almost daylight, and odd hosepipes drew their life blood from its unnoticed main water pipes. But along the Harbour behind me I had a message of the fires on the wharves, and looking up Clare Street I was appalled at the view of Wine Street. I could see All Saints' Church intact, but beyond the site of the old High Cross all detail was lost in one vast sheet of orange flame. I thought how, in peace time reporting, I had used the words "blazing inferno" and I lamented the paucity of the English

All that was left of the auditorium of the Regent Cinema in Castle Street following the raid of 24 November. *(Jim Facey)*

The gutted interior of Temple Church, Temple Street, looking from the tower towards the altar, as it looked following the raid of 24 November. *(Jim Facey)*

Looking up Castle Street from Old Market following the raid of 24 November. Tower Hill is off to the left. *(Jim Facey)*

language. I dropped in at the "Press" office, where the tape machines ticked steadily away in an air raid shelter. But what news had England for Bristol that night?'

'Further along Baldwin Street this tremendous story began all over again. Rowland Adams, the Fruiterer, on the corner of Queen Charlotte Street, was already a ruin, and I had a vague impression that parts of Queen Charlotte Street and the Welsh Back were burning. On the other side, 65 Baldwin Street, the Cunard – White Star offices, had taken the blow and at the end St. Nicholas Church shared the proud sacrifice of the secular buildings. On Bristol Bridge I stayed for a full five minutes. From there I had another impressive view of the Wine Street area. The whole block to Mary-le-Port Street was burning, and I guessed that Union Street and Narrow Wine Street were in very like plight. Straight through what had been the top of Bridge Street I saw the furnace that had been Castle Street – Castle Street, with the very new hiding the very old, where you could not drive your car on a Saturday night because of the crowd. With a sudden shock I realised that St Peter's Hospital and half the church had disappeared. My heart ached at the thought of that ever-young half-timbered front, and the age darkened oak of the panelled rooms, for these things meant much to me, as they did to most of you. I didn't mind so much the burning of the Regent Cinema next door, nor the carnage among the great stores further on, because they can be replaced. By the flames I followed the course of the water along the old Castle Moat and I thought of that great fire which had ravaged a walled city after the desolation of the mediaeval plague. But these fires were started by man himself.'

'Behind me the Avon was being pumped on to a great fire on the Redcliff water front, and away to the east of the city the sky repeated its tragic tale. I turned to the drama nearer at hand, Victoria Street. You know now, of course, that Robinson's on right and George's Brewery offices on the left made a flaming gateway to another trail of havoc that rivalled, and in parts surpassed the pity of Park Street. Yet I laughed as I entered that gate. High on a sturdy wall an automatic fire bell, fanned by the flames within, clanged with a regular, unmuffled beat. I approached an AFS man wiping the smuts from his eyes as he rested for a moment on his trailer pump. "Excuse me," I said, "but the bell's ringing. There must be a fire somewhere". Re-vitalised into action he sprang up. "Gosh – where?" he asked, and then took off his tin hat and rocked with laughter. Then: "D'you know, we've been trying to stop that ruddy bell for I don't know how long," and, still smiling, he returned to the fight'.

'Filled with admiration I lifted my bike and continued my insignificant way. Along most of Victoria Street, and in Temple Street too, when I made a forced detour, I protected my face with my hand from the sparks and the heat, and every now and then picked a singeing spark from my spray-damped clothes. But all around me these AFS fellows noticed nothing but the unremitting demands of their Herculean job. The worst spot was near Temple

Castle Street during the 1990s. *(Author's Collection)*

Church, where the aisle of the Weaver's Chapel was gone, but the solid tower leaned no more than of old. Already the place was unrecognisable, and the road itself was a mess such as a tornado might have made. From some unexpected stable carters and a couple of Blue-jackets were leading those familiar Bristol draught horses to safety, frightened, but unflinching, like the thoroughbreds they are. If ever a drama had a climax the tragedy of Victoria Street had that night. The vast furnace that had been Mardon's factories was a mighty valediction with a vengeance. The road I took then led to lesser scenes of destruction, fires and bomb craters, and the whole ARP service in gallant action, but always I turned back to look at the city itself.'

'When the "Raiders Passed" went I was back in Bristol, driving an Army lorry, instead of wheeling a bicycle, and before morning came I had side-tracked and detoured the pitted roads of Southville and Knowle and driven twice across the Suspension Bridge. What a sight we saw from there! The timber yards opposite Hotwells seemed to pale the spectacle of the other fires, and yet even as these were approached again they claimed the stage for themselves once more. That was the way it was last night. The senses could absorb so much and no more, and then they reeled. Even so, and this is worth noting, chaos never came, hard though it threatened. By the time Bristol breakfasted those fires were under control. Dawn saw the beginning of the salvage which soon set the wheels of the city moving again. The bombers have done their worst, but Bristol beat them, and will again!'

Above and Beyond the Call of Duty

One of the most difficult situations of the night occurred near Redcliff Hill, where two houses in Bryant Street had been completely demolished by a high-explosive bomb which also caused a fire, and it was here, while the residents of adjoining houses were being evacuated, that cries were heard coming from beneath the burning debris. Herbert Stanford, a Group Warden, immediately took charge of the situation and, while a fire pump was still playing water on the blaze, he worked his way through to the victims on his stomach and was soon able to give them a little water, along with much needed words of encouragement. As it was found impossible to get the trapped people out alive by removing the wreckage on top, it was decided to make a hole in the wall which divided the shattered building from the next house, but unfortunately when this had been done the rescuers were still unable to get through as their way was obstructed by debris. A temporary hold-up then ensued, but Stanford was not to be beaten and decided a way could be cleared by knocking out a fire grate. This was an awkward task, and it was three hours before it was possible to rescue a little boy alive and uninjured, followed half an hour later by a slightly older girl. The other four shelterers, however, were pinned down by debris and although during the hours it took to free them the building was still burning, coal gas was escaping and the raid was still going on above, the work continued unabated. An amazing rescue had been accomplished, and as a result of his outstanding bravery, initiative and perseverance and having set such a fine example that night, on 28 February 1941 Herbert Stanford was awarded the George Medal, and his portrait subsequently painted for the nation's war record.

Bridge Street looking down towards St Nicholas Church following the raid of 24 November. *(Jim Facey)*

The 24 November raid, engraved on the minds of Bristolians who lived through it for the amount of damage caused, dramatically highlighted the complete inability of the country's air defence system to protect the city from Luftwaffe bombers, and this was not helped by the fact that the new local 'Starfish' decoy sites had not been fired as the expert responsible could not be found! Something, therefore, had to be done quickly and so, in an attempt to provide a more adequate defence for Bristol, on 28 November a Flight of Hurricanes from No.87 Squadron, which was by then being used solely for night fighting, transferred from Exeter, via the still unserviceable new airfield at Colerne, to Charmy Down its satellite located just north of Bath,

Looking across what was once Bridge Street towards St Nicholas Church in the 1990s. *(Author's Collection)*

The Upper Arcade looking from St James's Barton towards the Horsefair following the raid of 24 November. *(Jim Facey)*

St James Barton as it was in the 1990s, looking towards the site of the old Upper Arcade. *(Author's Collection)*

although the other half of the squadron was not finally moved down from Bibury until mid-December.

Mercifully for British cities, extensive fog on the Continent ruled out any more large-scale raids on the nights immediately after the operation against Bristol, but with good weather still prevailing at Vannes airfield in Brittany an X-Verfahren assisted attack was mounted against Avonmouth by KGr 100 during the evening of 25 November. On this occasion the concentration point was the grain silos and cold stores in the Royal Edward Dock, and in spite of nine aircraft participating in the subsequent raid thick cloud over the target area ensured that the only serious incident to occur was a fire at the Shell Canning Factory. Although this was only a very minor attack, during the course of it the first 'Starfish' operation in Britain took place when the Chew Magna decoy was fired, but unfortunately it failed to attract any bombs. The following night, although fog was still widespread on the Continent, KGr 100 returned to Avonmouth with seven Heinkels, and once again the installations around the Royal Edward Dock were the concentration point. However, just as on the previous night thick cloud covered the target area, with only occasional clear intervals, and although the attackers all operated with X-Verfahren no significant damage was caused, the majority of the bombs falling harmlessly on open ground in the Avonmouth and Shirehampton areas.

CHAPTER 5

A BLEAK CHRISTMAS

December 1940

Unfortunately for Plymouth, London, Liverpool and Southampton the weather soon improved and all of these places were heavily raided in late November and early December, while Bristol was selected for a second major attack on the night of 2 December. Once again, however, bombing was to be restricted to the first half of the night to allow the participating aircraft to return to their bases before the onset of widespread fog in France. To guide KGr 100 to their target, during the afternoon the X-Beam stations near Cherbourg and Boulogne were ordered to align on the city's harbour facilities, but on this occasion a little upstream from the concentration point chosen on 24 November. In addition, just before nightfall the Knickebein transmitter at Dieppe, previously deployed over London, suddenly swung round and re-

Damage caused to the 6.10pm train from Bristol to Salisbury just as it was leaving Temple Meads station during the evening of 2 December. *(Jim Facey)*

aligned on Bristol to further assist the 132 aircraft taking part, a force made up of 69 Heinkels, 55 Junkers and 8 Dorniers from I. and III./KG1, I. and III./KG 27, I. and II./KG 54, I. and II./KG 55, KG 77, KGr 100, KGr 606, and II. and III./LG 1.

The general line of approach by the raiders was from the south, with a few odd aircraft coming in from the south-west, but when the leaders arrived they found there was nearly total cloud cover in two layers in the target area, the lower lying between 1,000 and 3,000ft, and the upper between 8,000 and 10,000ft, while underneath, surface visibility was poor, being down to just 3,000ft. As a result bombing was initially carried using Knickebein and 'Dead Reckoning' methods, causing a number of the parachute flares and incendiaries dropped by II./KG 55 at the start of the raid to fall over Clifton and the northern parts of the town. This prompted Oberleutnant Otto-Bernard Harms, Staffelkapitän of 4 Staffel, KG 55, to dive through both layers of cloud down to an altitude of only 1,000ft to check on the positioning of the gruppe's target marking fires and through this courageous action, carried out with complete disregard to the poor visibility, balloon barrage, and strong anti-aircraft fire, he was able to confirm the accuracy which many of his unit had achieved. Although later in the attack isolated breaks occurred in the cloud cover enabling some visual bombing to be carried, of the 121 crews who subsequently claimed to have dropped a total of 120.9 tonnes of high explosives, a tonne of oil bombs and 22,140 incendiaries on Bristol between 6.20 and 10.30pm, none were unable to provide an accurate assessment of the success of the operation.

As in the case of previous night attacks the Luftwaffe's losses had been minimal, amounting to a single Dornier 17 of KGr 606 which crashed soon after take-off from Brest, while poor weather had prevented much RAF fighter activity. Bristol's heavy guns had managed to fire some 4,556 rounds but all to no avail, and to make matters worse during the course of the raid a high-explosive bomb fell some 10yd from a Lewis gun emplacement on the Purdown heavy gun site wounding seven men of 236 Battery, 76th HAA Regiment. Two of these were seriously injured, one fatally, the first death from enemy action suffered by Bristol's anti-aircraft gunners. On a more positive note, damage to the balloon barrage was considerably less than on 24 November and amounted to just four envelopes punctured by bomb splinters and two operators slightly injured, while the two local 'Starfish' decoys were relatively successful, with Stockwood drawing 62 bombs and Chew Magna a further six.

Unknown to the Germans the damage caused to Bristol was of a more widespread nature than on 24 November, although the main concentration was astride a line running about due east and west through Redfield, St Paul's, Cotham

Whiteladies Road, corner of Burlington Road during the 1990s. (Author's Collection)

Bristol double decker bus FHT 98 damaged by blast at the corner of Whiteladies Road and Burlington Road following the raid of 2 December. Fortunately the bus was empty at the time. *(Jim Facey)*

Dean Street, St Paul's, looking towards Brigstocke Road, following the raid of 2 December. *(BUP)*

and Redland. The total number of incidents reported was 340, and although Bristol's ARP Services became fully extended it was not necessary to request reinforcements from outside the region. Rescue Parties were called to 66 occurrences, from which they brought out 135 persons alive and recovered 117 bodies, the most serious incident being at Dean Street, St Paul's, where a large calibre-bomb had detonated. On arrival the Rescue Party found the street to be completely blocked by large heaps of debris, a very large crater, and the collapse of several three-storey Georgian houses, one of which housed a Wardens' Post. Although 12 people were eventually rescued alive from the wreckage, 15 personnel from the

Dean Street, St Paul's during the 1990s. *(Author's Collection)*

Wardens' Post lost their lives, and it was to take 27 days to remove the bodies of all 40 of those who had perished.

During the following month their names were, of course, added to the growing casualty list, which finally revealed that in Bristol 156 people had been killed, and a further 270 treated for their injuries, either in hospital or at First Aid Posts. Others were more fortunate, and although a stick of high-explosive bombs caused extensive damage when it fell across the Bristol Children's Hospital on St Michael's Hill all 80 child patients and those on duty were safely evacuated within the space of just two hours. As during this time the behaviour of all those concerned was calm and professional, the hospital was subsequently presented with a framed appreciation by the Lord Mayor of Bristol, while on 25 April 1941 Gladys Ruth Ellis, the Matron, received a well-deserved MBE.

Once again the Fire Services were particularly busy, and of the 197 reported fires six were categorised serious and 76 medium, these being fought by a total of 409 pumps and 1,518 fire fighters, of which two, both AFS men, lost their lives. For the second time the local fire service was

Nurses busy evacuating children from Bristol Children's Hospital on St Michael's Hill following the raid of 2 December. *(BUP)*

completely overwhelmed, and at 6.52pm reinforcements were called in, some 63 brigades from Gloucestershire, Somerset, Wiltshire, Devon, Dorset, Oxfordshire, Berkshire, Monmouthshire, Warwickshire, Worcestershire, Buckinghamshire and South Wales subsequently despatching 94 pumps, 470 personnel and nearly 10,000ft of additional hose to Bristol, ensuring that shortly before daybreak the fires were all under control.

One man who took an active part in protecting Bristol from the menace of the incendiary bombs was 30-year-old Bill Hares, who lived with his wife and two children above the family confectionery and tobacco shop in Merchant Street, close to the city centre. Although the shop was shut-up through supply shortages, Bill and his family got by reasonably well, looked after by firms for whom he acted as a Fire Watcher, in spite of the fact that he only had one leg! That night Bill wrote in his diary,

'Siren goes. I'm listening to the News, but the gun-fire is very heavy. Look out and see flares dropping over Clifton way. My other two mates have left us in the lurch again. Only two of us to look after three buildings. Have to make the wife take shelter. Tell her we're in for another pasting. Plenty of planes in the sky. Intermittent gun-fire. Tell a young lady to take cover. Give same warning to a young man and his girl-friend, who seem very frightened, but who says that she has only to die once. Pick up with a deaf fellow, and ask him to lend a hand. He's quite willing, and shows no fear. He's been to sea and has been torpedoed. Just the right man in a pinch!'

'Bombs dropping nearer now. Have to lay down several times. Somehow, though, it's not like the first night. I suppose the thought of getting through one blitz makes it an odds-on chance of seeing this lot over. Big blaze in the middle of town, and Jerries seem to be concentrating on that. Bombs whistling down. Funny to see the deaf man fall down when I do, like a one-man act. There's a very close one! We're covered with blue sparks. Everything seems to rock. Fires are now blazing in Stokes Croft, North Street and the middle of town. Someone tells me that Temple Meads Station has copped it and that most of the early stuff fell Westbury way. Barrage intermittent. Not so continuous as the first blitz. Then we get some excitement in our sector. Incendiaries fall across the Quaker's Friar's roof, and the beams start to blaze. I go and tell them what has happened as there is a lot burning round the garage petrol pumps, I cycle round to the Wardens' Post to report it. Return to find the caretaker and a policeman, silhouetted against the red glow of a big fire across Newfoundland Street, taking no notice of the stuff that is falling. Policeman shouts to the caretaker to pump harder. Then a swish, another string of incendiaries comes sailing down across the road. We think they have missed us, and go across the road to see where they have fallen.'

'Glory be! Our own building's ablaze. I didn't know what to think for a moment. The fire seems to be out of control in a few minutes. I shout to "Deaffy" to follow me, and we rush up the stairs. Fire has caught the beams and there is the sound of hissing. "Deaffy" starts to put out the flames on the second floor with his foot and cap. I rush to the top floor and let the bomb there have it with a bucketful of water. The worst thing I could have done, for the whole thing went up in a sheet of white flame. Fire seemed to spread all around me. I got panicky, and started to back away. Fell over a bucket of sand. Threw sand on to the fire, and was surprised to see the flames die down. "Deaffy" has now stamped and almost put out the fire on the second floor; we got to work with stirrup pump, and in no time it seemed that the job was finished. So I stuck out my chest.'

'The fires tonight seem to have got under control much quicker than I thought they would. Practice must make perfect. Harris's across the road starts to burn. Flames coming from the glass fanlight. Looks like a big fire. Dash round to the Wardens' Post, but a messenger is already on the way. On returning, a Jerry plane comes in low and lets go his load of hate. It falls quite near, and my bike seems to be sucked across the road. Another explosion. Phew! That's a close one. Auxiliaries on the job pretty quickly. Not long before water is being pumped on to the flames. But another building is doomed. Another big fire for Jerry to play on. Again we are between two fires, because the Dockland Settlement in Rosemary Street and buildings beyond are blazing. But despite to-night's fires, there is not the same excitement as there was on the first night's blitz. Things are easing off and we now wait for the "All Clear".'

To keep up the pressure on the British population, the following day the Germans stepped up the propaganda war, their official communiqué announcing to the world that;

'Strong units of the German Air Force crossed the Channel last night to attack Bristol to complete the work of destroying industrial and port installations as at Coventry and Southampton. Our bombardment of Coventry opened a new phase of industrial warfare; attacks on Coventry, Liverpool, Southampton, Bristol and Birmingham will be followed by others on other cities.'

Bristol's Third Attack Within a Fortnight

The enemy's chilling warning certainly needed to be taken seriously for in spite of the fact that during the next few nights Birmingham and Plymouth were singled out for attention, on the evening of 6 December Bristol's third large raid within a fortnight took place. To begin with all went well for the Luftwaffe, and although during the afternoon the X-Beam stations near Cherbourg and Boulogne were busy aligning on the same concentration point as that used for the previous operation, at 4.05pm they were ordered to switch off as gale force west to north-west winds in northern France meant that KGr 100 would have to remain grounded. Nevertheless, Knickebein

The Merchant's Hall, Marsh Street, following the raid of 6 December. *(BUP)*

transmissions monitored during the early evening gave British intelligence an indication that Bristol was to be attacked, but fortunately the adverse weather ensured that as well as KGr 100, a number of other units were also unable to participate. Consequently, a force of only 41 Heinkels and 39 Junkers supplied by II./KG 27, I. and II./KG 51, I.,II. and III./KG 55, KG 77 and I. and II./LG 1 set off to bomb Bristol, of which just 67 subsequently reported attacking the city with 77.5 tonnes of high explosives, half a tonne of oil bombs, and 5688 incendiaries on the city between 7.20 and 10.45pm.

As a result of the non-appearance of KGr 100 the raid was undertaken without precision radio assisted pathfinders and was opened by II./KG 55 dropping marker flares, a number of which were carried away to the east in the strong westerly wind. The direction from which the attack was made was also quite different to that used during previous operations, the raiders following a line from Shaftesbury to Bath, and when east of Bristol turning due west to drop their bombs across the city from east to west. In the target area it was extremely cold, but fine and moonlit with 10 per cent cloud cover at about 2,500ft and this good visibility, marred by only a small amount of broken cloud, permitted visual bombing with the result that the operation was considered to have been carried out successfully. Yet again losses were acceptable, and although no aircraft failed to return a Heinkel from II./KG 27 and two Ju 88s, one belonging to III./KG 77 and the other to I./KG 51, all crashed on their return to France.

Sadly in Bristol it was a different story, and during the course of the attack 100 people were killed and 188 injured, with much of the damage being caused by fire. The areas mainly affected were in the vicinity of St Philip's Marsh, Temple Meads, the city centre and Cotham, and Rescue Parties were sent to 34 occurrences from which 38 persons were rescued alive and 61 bodies recovered. However, in spite of the carnage all 110 patients in the Bristol General Hospital escaped injury when two high explosives fell so close to the building that hundreds of its windows were blown out, their lives having been saved by the staff who had started moving them to safer parts of the hospital as soon as the alert sounded. A group of smiling nurses said afterwards that the patients; 'All behaved splendidly and no one even murmured, though some were very ill', while the hospital's chairman added that; 'It is impossible to speak too highly of the work done by the staff'.

Once again the incendiary bombs proved very effective, and a total of 104 fires were started, of which 11 were minor, 43 small, 45 medium and five serious, forcing the city to request Regional reinforcements at 7.59pm, some 32 brigades subsequently arriving in Bristol from Gloucestershire, Somerset, Wiltshire, and Devon, a deployment that enabled all the fires to be brought under control by 4.30 the next morning. Although the overall situation was not as serious as in the previous two large-scale attacks, by the end of the night three AFS men had lost their lives and another had been detained in hospital suffering from severe lacerations. By contrast, the Civil Defence Services suffered only one fatality, but in this case the circumstances were particularly tragic as the unfortunate lady involved, Dorothy Cook of the WVS who had been on continual duty for a week, was drowned when her Mobile Canteen plunged into the docks, trapping her in the vehicle.

Bill Hares down in Merchant Street was once again in the thick of the action, as his diary reveals: 'Warning. Gunfire heavy. Plenty of planes about. Some flares dropped but it seems the Jerries are after something else tonight. Then Fire Watcher calls out to us to observe a plane in the searchlights. Planes are very low tonight. Some damned good pilots, I should think. Flares over Temple Meads. We are all waiting for something to happen. More planes, swarms of them, although they seem to be passing over the town, and leaving us alone. Everyone appears to be on tip-toe tonight. Now a Jerry makes a smoke sign. Think at first it has been hit by the AA, but it passes out of sight. More flares. Still no action. Then we get a thrill. Two planes come in, one with smoke pouring from its tail; the other behind it with navigation lights full on. They pass over, and the first plane makes a complete circle of white smoke.'

'A few incendiaries fall. One near the Mail Coach, and a War Reserve Constable takes a flying kick at it. It's soon put out. Then comes the heavy stuff. There is a glow in the sky from the docks, and over Temple Meads and Redcliff way fires start to burn furiously. We wait for more incendiaries, though there seems little doing in our particular neighbourhood. City Mill catches fire, but firemen are soon on the job. It's blazing fiercely. Firemen told of manholes in the street, and they get to work quickly, and soon have the pumps going. Jerry is still coming over, but there seems to be several minute intervals between the planes. Wife gets firemen some tea but they are too busy to drink it. A big and heavy direct hit on the little Gem Cinema is scored. Luckily the Fire Watcher had moved away in time. Tonight it seems that most of the fires are quickly under control, and everybody carried on just as a matter of fact. If a big 'un falls near, they joke about it, and people are out in the streets watching the fire fighters. City Mill now well under control, but there's a big fire in Bridge Street. Early "All Clear".'

Desperate Times Call for Desperate Measures

In another attempt to thwart the Luftwaffe, at the beginning of December a new experiment in night defence began in which Handley Page Hampden bombers based in Lincolnshire started flying defensive patrols for the close protection of a number of important industrial centres. The operation of these so called 'Interception Patrols' required the improvised fighters to fly within a ten mile radius of the centre of the target city for some four hours, during which time it was arranged that no anti-aircraft guns were to engage, or searchlights expose in the patrol area. As it transpired the night of 6 December was the only occasion on which the Hampdens operated over Bristol, but in spite of some 20 aircraft from No.44 and No.49 Squadrons at Scampton patrolling from 10.45pm until 1.20am, no contact was made with the enemy. The city's heavy anti-aircraft gunners again put up a spirited defence, firing a total of 1,013 rounds before the Hampdens arrived, but they also failed to engage the enemy, while for a second time in three days a bomb scored a direct hit on one

The Predictor pit on the Purdown gun site as it was in the 1990s. *(Author's Collection)*

of Bristol's gun sites. On this occasion Brickfields was involved, the high-explosive detonating under the concrete foundations of a gun which had been firing a only few moments before, silencing the weapon and injuring two men of 238 Battery, 76th HAA Regiment. The night, however, was not a complete disaster as the city's passive defences proved somewhat more successful, the Stockwood decoy site attracting 73 bombs which might otherwise have caused serious damage or loss of life in the nearby conurbation.

After two more unsuccessful 'Interception Patrols' elsewhere in the country, it was realised that the Hampden night fighter experiment was a complete failure, and so before the middle of the

month it was terminated to be replaced with concentrated patrols of 'Cats Eye' single-engined fighters flying over potential targets, a system initially code named 'Operation Layers', but which in April 1941 was renamed 'Fighter Nights'. The first three serious night attacks on

The Rangefinder pit on the Purdown gun site as it was in the 1990s. *(Author's Collection)*

Bristol had also revealed a number of shortcomings in the local heavy anti-aircraft defence layout, so in order to allow more guns to fire linear barrages over the south of the city, in mid-December four 3.7" mobiles were sent to the then empty Whitchurch gun site.

Starting to Feel the Strain

Back in mid-November 1940 Bristol had appeared well prepared for anything the Luftwaffe might have in store for them, and even the minority of those citizens who had anticipated heavier attacks were beginning to feel that after all things might not be too serious, and that even preparations undertaken on their behalf were adequate. Nevertheless, the failure of the locals to learn from the experience of people in such places as London and Coventry was something observers found somewhat disturbing. The horror of the first three heavy raids therefore came as an unpleasant shock to many Bristolians, and when on 9 December the Mass Observation 'blitz team' arrived in the city they noted that people were coping far less well than those in a similar situation in other parts of the country. It was recorded that: 'They were particularly cheerless and, unlike at Southampton, failed to make any jokes about the raids, having preferred to gather morbidly for weeks around the bomb-sites, indulging in defeatist talk and spreading numerous rumours.'

It was also found that locally there was a particularly keen following for the nightly *Views on the News* broadcasts made by William Joyce, better known as 'Lord Haw Haw' which were transmitted from Germany immediately after the BBC's own 9pm news bulletin, while at the same time the Regional Information Office in Bristol reported deep disillusion with BBC bulletins, largely because these were regarded as giving insufficient credit to the sufferings of the locals. One of the odd by-products of wartime censorship was the development of what is best described as a league table of suffering in

A lady stops for a smoke on the rubble of what was once a Bristolians home. *(Jim Facey)*

A chef from Jones's wrecked department store in a defiant mood amid the ruins of Mary-le-Port Street following the raid of 24 November. *(Jim Facey)*

provincial cities, and although only a few days before the 24 November attack newsreels showing the destruction of Coventry had been shown in local cinemas, Bristol's big raid received no similar publicity and this, not surprisingly, caused a certain amount of bad feeling in the city.

The Mass Observation team went on to report that: 'The damage in Bristol was considerably less than in Coventry and Southampton and that the public utilities were working well, with the telephone system practically back to normal'. They found nothing like the dislocation and multiplied personal discomfort which still dominated private and domestic life in Southampton or Coventry, as for the first time in a provincial 'blitz' hot meals had been quickly made available. Nevertheless, in spite of all this, there seemed to be more depression in Bristol than had been found in any of the other bombed cities recently visited, with open defeatism being encountered, especially among younger workers, and much wishful thinking about the war being over.

On a more positive note, it was found that there was a 'Remarkably low degree of private evacuation and desertion', for the working classes, in particular, had overwhelmingly stayed put, in stark contrast to the situation at Coventry and Southampton. This was quite surprising, as Bristol had a public shelter system felt by many locally to be totally inadequate, a feeling which had been aggravated by the fact that many shelters had been demolished and rebuilt in full public view, and these included many made of brick and cement which had been insufficiently mortared when originally constructed. To quote Mass Observation's December report:

> 'There is a violent minority dissatisfaction with Bristol's shelters, and this is certainly often
> spontaneous, non-political, and actually justified. Investigators with a wide comparison of
> experience with town shelter facilities consider these in Bristol to be strikingly inferior and
> inadequate in many parts of the town.'

Bristol did, however, have two big advantages, for not only was it a large conurbation, much less concentrated than the other southern coastal towns, but it was also the designated centre for the Region, which ensured that the Regional Commissioner, Sir Hugh Elles, was nearly always on the spot to react quickly inside the local lines of intercommunication which he had personally established in preceding months.

A Brace of Local Heroes

During the second week of December the Germans turned their attention to London, while on the night of the 11, some 290 bombers from Luftflotte 3 took off to attack Birmingham, 42 of which for various reasons were forced to make for alternative targets, a Dornier 17 from KGr 606 and a Heinkel 111 from III./KG 27 selecting Bristol, while a Junkers 88 from I./LG 1 made for Avonmouth. The first to attack was the Dornier which at 8.25pm released its bomb load of ten 50kg high explosives and 60 incendiaries across Bristol, the bombs subsequently falling in Lawrence Hill, St Philips, the Central area, Montpelier, St Augustine's, Redland and St Anne's, killing one person and injuring eight others. This was followed at 10.30pm by the Junkers which dropped its two bombs, one a 250kg and the other a 1,000kg on Shirehampton, injuring seven people. The Heinkel was the last to attack but it seems to have been somewhat disorientated, as its four bombs dropped at 10.55pm all came down over 30 miles away in the vicinity of Gloucester and Newent!

42 Bath Buildings, Montpelier, following the raid of 11 December. It was here that ARP Rescue Party Leader, William Atkin won his BEM.

One of the high explosives dropped by the Dornier scored a direct hit on a house and general store in Bath Buildings, Montpelier, killing one person, injuring three others, and carving the building clean out of its rank while leaving the neighbouring party walls practically intact. As a result, three of the occupants were trapped beneath the wreckage, while beneath them coal gas was escaping from the service pipe which, because of the amount of rubble in the road, proved impossible to isolate for a considerable time. Upon the arrival of the Rescue Party the cries of the trapped were heard from under the debris and, as removal of this from the top was inadvisable, Party Leader William Atkin at once began work to break an opening from the cellar of an adjoining house through a 20in wall. In spite of the cellar being full of escaping gas, the rescuers, by working in relays, succeeded in making an opening large enough to remove obstacles, through which two people were rescued alive, and one body recovered.

In the house when the bomb struck were Mr McGrath, Mrs Caroline Wadman who was killed, her sister, and a young man who lodged there. Within seconds, Mr McGrath who was in the bathroom at the time, had been blown a distance of about 15ft, out through the wall and into the garden, where he was found lying dazed and severely bruised, but otherwise unhurt. Mr Comer later recalled that when the Rescue Squad arrived:

'We started knocking a hole through the house next door and had got through when we realised that it was dangerous to proceed as the chimney breast was leaning precariously. We then proceeded to dig our way through the cellar, and luckily hit upon the cellar of the bombed house. We had to go in on our hands and knees, each taking a turn, but there was a serious escape of gas which forced us to come out every few minutes for fresh air. We soon came across the young lodger trapped among the rubble. He was dazed but did not appear to be seriously injured. After he had been taken away by ambulance we continued to tunnel further into the house and heard moans and cries of a woman, these led us in the right direction. We came across an armchair and a lot of other timber which blocked the way. Owing to the smallness of the hole nobody seemed able to move it.'

'I told the head of the Rescue Squad that I was left handed and might stand a better chance of removing the obstacle. I went in with a saw and sawed it in half and managed to clear it out of the way. I came across the woman just afterwards. She was dazed and said to

Training for rescue from a basement. *(NFS)*

me, "My poor sister, she is just behind me". I didn't know how I was going to bring her out. I pulled her on top of me and wriggled backwards through the tunnel carrying her with me on my stomach. I was feeling ill from the effects of gas by this time, but an Ambulance man revived me. We carried on to look for Mrs Wadman and came across her pinned under debris. It was obvious that she was dead. We could not get her out the same way, so I started digging from the top and finally got her body out. Before that I remembered where the gas main was and decided to have a go at stopping the leakage. I dug down in the front garden and came to the gas main, which I hammered together and stopped the leak. The rescue work went more quickly after that.'

Several of the rescue men were, however, taken ill as a result of the noxious effects of coal gas, and the squad leader collapsed later from the same cause and was subsequently retained in hospital for a whole week. It therefore came as no surprise to those who had assisted with the rescue work when, on 21 February 1941, it was announced that William Herbert Atkin, their leader, was to receive the British Empire Medal for his selfless actions under the most difficult of circumstances.

While all this was going on at 10.32pm a telephone message was received by the Bristol Fire Brigade stating that at Day's Road, St Philips the top of the smaller gas holder had been penetrated and the coal gas set on fire by incendiary bombs. Although George Jones, who worked for the Bristol Gas Company, was not on duty that night he immediately went to the scene of the fire, and with the assistance of other employees, very pluckily attacked the seat of the blaze and ultimately succeeded in sealing the gas holder with clay and a metal plate. This had the effect of stopping the escaping gas, and as a result the fire itself was extinguished in about an hour by the use of a standpipe and six lengths of hose. For this and his previous courageous action during the evening of 24 November, when he had also extinguished an incendiary on a gas holder, George Jones was awarded the George Medal on 2 May 1941.

Fortunately for Bristolians, from mid-December until early January 1941 their city was free from the unwanted attention of the Luftwaffe's bombers as they were busy operating over other British targets, while just before the end of the year the Junkers 88s of LG 1 were transferred out of Luftflotte 3 and down to the Mediterranean theatre. Unfortunately, in spite the loss of some 80 aircraft, when the attackers did return they had in fact received a considerable boost, the decision having been made to make available the bomber units of Luftflotte 2 to assist Luftflotte 3 with operations over Western Britain. This was to be a considerable help as this force numbered some 400 aircraft, made up of the Heinkel 111s of KG 4, KG 28, and KG 53, as well as the Junkers 88s of KG 30 and the Dornier 17s of KG 2 and KG 3.

CHAPTER 6

A MISERABLE NEW YEAR

January and February 1941

Unfortunately, the New Year of 1941 brought no respite to beleaguered Bristol, for not only had additional bombers been made available to carry out attacks on the area, but the unfortunate defenders also had to cope with dreadful weather conditions. During the first week of January North-West Europe was dominated by an anti-cyclone centred over the North Sea, with a ridge of high pressure extending south-westwards over Britain. This brought bitterly cold north-easterly winds and snow to much of the country, while at night clearing skies ensured that temperatures in many areas fell well below freezing. Nevertheless, in spite of the intense cold the night of 3 January 1941 saw the first combined operation carried out by 202 aircraft drawn from both Luftflotte 2 and Luftflotte 3, their task being 'to complete the destruction of the harbour

The wreckage of 21 Sion Road, Bedminster, showing two brothers digging in vain to rescue their mother, Florence Doggett, following the raid of 3 January. *(Jim Facey)*

The remains of the Scholastic store at the corner of High Street and Bridge Street following the raid of 3 January. *(Jim Facey)*

installations, large mills, warehouses and cold stores in Bristol, in order to paralyse it as a large trading centre supplying Southern England.' To accomplish this Luftflotte 3 dispatched I. and III./KG 1, I. and III./KG 26, I. and II./KG 27, I. and II./KG 54, I.,II. and III./KG 55, I. and III./KG 77, KGr 100, and I./LG 1, some 125 aircraft in all, while Luftflotte 2 contributed elements of KG 2, KG 3, KG 4, KG 30 and KG 53. This was to be the largest scale raid attempted against the city during World War Two, and the concentration point for the attack, the city centre on both sides of the River Avon, was similar to that chosen for the two raids carried out in December. British radio monitors were also busy that night, and as a result of their intercepts were able to deduce that the first of the raiders was expected to reach Bristol around 6.30pm via a beam transmitted by the Cherbourg Knickebein station.

The attack was opened by Luftflotte 3 which subsequently operated 111

From High Street looking up what remained of Bridge Street during the 1990s. *(Author's Collection)*

Stafford Street, Bedminster, following the raid of 3 January. *(Jim Facey)*

aircraft over Bristol between 6.35pm and 0.38am, with a second wave of 67 bombers from Luftflotte 2 bombing between 1.40 and 5.51am, a total 152 tonnes of high explosives, two tonnes of oil bombs and 53,568 incendiaries, being dropped over the target during the longest raid that Bristolians had yet suffered. To being with many aircraft appeared to meander about after crossing the British coast and some early arrivals from KG 1 circled the Bristol area while awaiting the arrival of the pathfinder Heinkels from KGr 100, which had been delayed in taking off from Vannes because of weather conditions. Likewise, their colleagues from III./KG 26 were even later arriving over the city, so on this occasion all bombed visually and not by means of their usual Y-Verfahren.

Three distinct directions of approach were used by the attackers, the first passing over Southampton, the second via Portland, and the third, employed by aircraft from Luftflotte 2, by way of Clacton on Sea. Although for the most part the bombers used one line of attack at a time, towards the end of the raid all three approaches seemed to be in use at the same time with aircraft converging on Bristol with remarkable precision. Locally, it was a very cold night with a clear starlit sky, and at the start of the raid both the city with a covering of snow and the course of the River Avon, were both clearly visible in the moonlight. The amount of cloud cover then began to increase as the night progressed, but breaks still permitted a degree of visual bombing, although recourse to Knickebein and 'Dead Reckoning' was necessary from time to time until the fires had developed sufficiently to be used as aiming points. So intense did some of the conflagrations become, that after midnight

Stafford Street, Bedminster, following the raid of 3 January. *(Jim Facey)*

burning Bristol could be seen by returning crews from a distance of around 100 miles. From the Luftwaffe's point of view it had been another successful operation, especially as the only casualty they suffered was a Dornier 17 from III./KG 3 which was damaged while crash landing on return to St Trond-Brusthem airfield in Belgium, while in a parallel operation the Heinkels from I./KG 28 managed to sow twelve mines in the shipping channels in the Severn Estuary.

During the night Fighter Command, with some degree of optimism, instituted 'Operation Layers' over Bristol for the first time, but in spite of such a large number of enemy aircraft flying over the area the sole claim of a Junkers 88 damaged at 21,000ft above the city by a Hurricane of No.87 Squadron was as near as the British fighters came to success. Unfortunately, the heavy anti-aircraft guns fared little better and, in spite of expending 1,317 rounds while the interceptors were not patrolling, no tangible results were obtained. Local decoys were also fired and, while the Chew Magna 'Starfish' did collect six high explosives and about a thousand incendiaries, the Stockwood site failed to attract a single bomb. In Bristol, the principal areas affected were Bedminster, St Philip's, Hotwells and Cotham, with both Temple Meads railway station and the City Docks sustaining a certain amount of damage, and had so many buildings in the centre of the city not been previously demolished, this would probably have proved more destructive than any of the previous raids. Some 150 incidents were subsequently plotted at ARP Control, but the actual number was greatly in excess of this as, owing to a modification in routine as a result of the experience of former raids, minor incidents causing neither damage nor casualties, were no longer being reported. Although casualties were less than on 24 November, in Bristol a total of 149 people were killed and 315 injured, in spite of the fact that German instructions regarding the target had been intercepted and decoded well before the raid began.

A Dreadful Night for the Emergency Services

As the night was one of the winter's bitterest, the lot of the fire-fighters was perhaps the worst, for as water streamed from their jets huge icicles formed on the buildings they were trying to save, while great sheets of ice on the roadways added to their misery. The brave and spirited women of the WVS who had taken their canteens out with refreshments for the hard-pressed emergency services also suffered terribly, and as one of the ladies later recalled; 'The firemen put the cups with dregs down and they froze. The tea froze. The hose froze. We had a choice of being frozen, burned, blown up, or drowned in tea!' With so many problems in Bristol, some 60 fire brigades were soon being ordered to the city from Gloucestershire, Somerset, Devon, Hampshire, Oxfordshire, Berkshire, Buckinghamshire and Surrey, and through this action much property was saved. Nevertheless, eight local firemen, two Fire Watchers, a Police War Reserve Constable and an Ambulance Driver, made the ultimate sacrifice that night, and it was particularly tragic that the eight fire-fighters, as well as the policeman, all died together in High Street where a long drawn out struggle had taken place to save the Posada Restaurant. At first it had seemed that the battle might be won, but

Water from firemen's hoses froze into long icicles on this escape ladder during the raid of 3 January. *(Jim Facey)*

Icicles hanging from the remains of the Corporation Granary on Princes Wharf following the raid of 3 January. *(Jim Facey)*

The wreckage of the YWCA Hostel, 14 Berkeley Square, following the raid of 3 January. Here rescue parties spent many days recovering trapped people and bodies. *(BUP)*

towards midnight the bombers came over again to complete the work of destruction. Nevertheless, in spite of high-explosive bombs falling all around the area, four firemen and two soldiers continued to pour water onto the burning building until a heavy explosion at the back of Oliver's shop on the opposite side of the road sent burning debris in all directions, and brought down a number of nearby buildings. Within the blink of an eye both Oliver's and the Posada had been blasted flat and the firemen on the roof blown off, while those standing in the road were buried under tons of fallen masonry. So large was the pile of rubble that it was just before noon the following day before rescue workers digging amid the ruins found the bodies of two Auxiliary Firemen and a soldier, but it took many more hours to shift the rest of the debris and recover all the pitiful human remains.

The Rescue Parties were also busy elsewhere, the other major occurrence being in Berkeley Square where several days were spent recovering trapped persons and 15 bodies from the YWCA Hostel. Others were more lucky and for the second time the Bristol General Hospital had a narrow escape, in spite of the fact that on this occasion a large number of incendiaries destroyed a top floor nurses quarters, three wards below and the hospital's dome, while high explosives impacting nearby blew out many of the windows. Nevertheless, although conditions in the building were almost beyond description, with water and filth cascading down through ceilings, staircases, lift shafts and air-ducts, all the patients were evacuated uninjured to temporary accommodation elsewhere in the city. Throughout the raid Annie Caroline Robins, the Matron, showed the utmost devotion to duty and set an outstanding example of fortitude and courage to her staff and for that, as well as her actions during the previous attack, she was awarded an OBE on 9 May 1941.

Bill Hares diary entry for that night recorded that,

'there is a very heavy barrage and planes are coming in low, and swiftly. Flares drop over Easton way. More over city centre. Warn people in street to expect something pretty soon, and tell them to get water and pumps ready. Incendiaries drop in Broad Weir, and a colleague chases off against my orders and flings a bucket of water over one. Up she goes in a sheet of flame. His clothes are burnt and he hurts his side'.

'Street Fire Watchers are chasing about and doing good work all over the place. Then down across the street and buildings falls another string of incendiaries. Several are on Quaker's Friars, more around the garage. Plenty are burning in the street and one is burning on the Coroner's Court". Our buildings are apparently all right. So I smash in the Coroner's

The Bedminster Tram Depot at Sheene Road following the raid of 3 January. *(Jim Facey)*

Court window and then realise it's a very high roof and has got to be tackled from outside. No ladder about, so I have to climb the drainpipe. Get a shovel, tie it on my walking stick, then shin up the drainpipe, and clamber on to the roof. By now two other men are out and getting the water ready. The incendiary is fizzing away merrily, and I start shovelling it over the tiles bit by bit. It's a very poor bomb with hardly any kick in it, although if left it could have caused another fire. One of the men hands me up a bucket of water and I succeed in putting out the burning woodwork. Getting off the roof is a darn sight more difficult, and the water has now frozen and the tiles are one sheet of ice. Keep thinking of the iron spiked railings in case I should slip! Very nasty work. Big fires across the river. Appears that the

docks are the main object tonight. Jones's in Broadmead is burning but the firemen are soon there, and I think it will soon be out. The water is freezing, as it leaks from the hoses. Very difficult to get about. The "All Clear" goes.'

High Street looking from Bristol Bridge following the raid of 3 January. On the right is the ruins of the Scholastic store, with what remained of the Posada behind United Clothiers premises. *(BUP)*

Looking up High Street during the 1990s. *(Author's Collection)*

'A second warning. Now for the heavy stuff, think I, and I'm not far wrong. It seems Jerry has altered his tactics, for now aircraft come in very low; drop one H.E. and then scoot like the devil away from the barrage. Some very good target bombing tonight and he's not wasting many. Although we are on the edge of the target area and the big ones are whining down quite regularly, you have a feeling that your own district will not get it. The factory is shaken several times, and there is a great mushroom of smoke and debris from a large bomb that lands in the ruins at the top of Bridge Street. Barrage seems to make everything vibrate and we wonder when it is going to end. The docks and Redcliff Street are one blazing mass, providing Jerry with a wonderful target, and doesn't he play on it! Hour

Bridge Street from the corner of Baldwin Street and Welsh Back following the raid of 3 January. *(Jim Facey)*

after hour it goes on, although the planes are now not so persistent. The monotony of it makes me tired. Some of the watchers pack up and go home. You feel there will be no more incendiaries to deal with and I get in the chair for forty winks. The place is rocked by a very near one. So it goes on. The "All Clear" goes and so ends our first all night blitz.'

The Luftwaffe's First Big Failure

The Bristol area had indeed been badly mauled, and to make matters worse a follow-up attack by 165 aircraft was also attempted against Avonmouth on the night of 4 January, the concentration point being centered on the docks and industrial installations situated in the western and northern parts of the town. On this occasion the participating units from Luftflotte 3 were I./KG 26, I. and II./KG 27, I., II. and III./KG 51, I. and II./KG 54, II. and III./KG 77, and KGr 100, while from Luftflotte 2 came elements of KG 2, KG 3, KG 4, KG 30 and KG 53. However, unlike on the previous afternoon the RAF's radio monitoring service was unable to give any early warning of an impending attack, and it was not until 6.45pm that the Kleve Knickebein was finally detected when it laid a beam over the Thames Estuary to guide Luftflotte 2's navigators to Bristol.

In spite of the bitter cold the weather at the start of the attack was moderately good with about 80 per cent cloud at about 5,000ft and a bright moon, so the first formations arriving over the target were, in some cases, able to bomb visually. Nevertheless, as the attack progressed thick cloud cover did develop after which bombing was principally by 'Dead Reckoning' and Knickebein, or by using the previously kindled fires as aiming points. The thick clouds also made it difficult to assess the overall results, and only after midnight were light flickering fires reported in the Avonmouth Dock area. In spite of the deteriorating weather conditions once again no German aircraft were actually lost, the only casualty being a Dornier 17 of I./KG 2 which was damaged during a crash landing back at its airfield at Cambrai-Epinoy, while for the second time a successful parallel operation had been carried out by I./KG 28 which laid 14 mines in the Severn Estuary.

Although the crews of the 127 aircraft which subsequently reported over Avonmouth and Bristol claimed during de-briefing to have dropped a total of 106.5 tonnes of high explosives, 1.5 tonnes of oil bombs and 27,722 incendiaries between 6.35pm and 6.15am, the raid had actually failed to develop, and although a number of fires were caused in buildings of national importance at Avonmouth, effective fire fighting ensured that most had been extinguished by 10pm. This deprived later arrivals of any aiming points, causing the subsequent bombing to creep down the Bristol Channel coast, past Clevedon, and on to Weston-super-Mare where a sharp attack took place. So it was that in the Bristol area only two people were killed and five injured that night, while sadly at Weston 34 died and a further 85 were wounded as a result of the five high explosives and the 3,000 or so incendiaries which fell across the town.

Bristol's Wonderful Beaufighter

The New Year of 1941 saw the British air defence system still practically impotent, but all this was about to change as a most important improvement in its capability took place during early January when the first local medium-range precision Ground Controlled Interception radar station came into operation at Avebury, in Wiltshire. GCI stations, which were designed to guide the pilot of a Beaufighter to the general vicinity of a raider, quickly proved successful and others were subsequently opened elsewhere in the South and West, at last providing some degree of protection for Bristol, South Wales and the industrial Midlands. Although the powerful twin-engined Bristol Beaufighter, brought into service to replace the obsolete Blenheim, was fast, heavily armed, and fitted with the latest and most effective Airborne Interception radar equipment yet devised, serious supply problems still existed in early 1941. However, the new GCI system did allow those aircraft already in service to operate on the Luftwaffe's main approach routes, thereby leaving the locally based Hurricanes free to fly an 'Operation Layers' over Bristol, and two such operations were to be undertaken in January during attacks on the city.

Snow, low cloud, freezing drizzle, sleet and rain over much of Britain and the Continent meant that for nearly a week Luftwaffe operations were drastically scaled down, but better weather between 9 and 15 January ensured that the night bombers were again active, this time over Manchester, London, Portsmouth, Plymouth and Derby. Also during this period, in spite of heavy cloud cover over the area, German photographic reconnaissance finally revealed that Avonmouth had been virtually undamaged by the 4 January raid, and so it was singled out for further attention. This also fitted in well with new instructions issued on 13 January by the High Command of the German Armed Forces which directed that the attacks still being carried out against the industrial centres of Britain were to be scaled down in favour of an all-out night-time assault on the vital importing harbours, the approaches to which were also to be regularly mined. Additionally, it was also considered important that key points of the air armaments and aircraft industry should be subjected to 'Pirate' attacks by single aircraft during daylight hours whenever suitable cloud cover was available.

Avonmouth Revisited

The follow-up Avonmouth, attack, which took place on the night of January 16th was to have the town and northern part of the dock area and its industrial installations as its concentration point, while in a parallel operation two lone Junkers 88s from I./KG 51 were also briefed to bomb Parnall Aircraft plant at Yate and Gloster Aircraft at Brockworth. Unlike the situation on 4 January, for this raid Luftflotte 3 were to operate alone, the attack force of 178 aircraft being drawn from III./KG 26, I., II. and III./KG 27, I., II. and III./KG 51, I. and II./KG 54, Stab, I., II. and III./KG 55, KGr 100, KGr 806, and I./LG 1. Although both X and Y-Verfahren were in operation, an X-Beam signal failure and winds stronger than forecast made KGr 100's bombing uncertain, although flares were again dropped early in the attack by II./KG 55 and again at 1.45am by II./KG 54, when a second phase began.

The first formations over the target encountered 80 per cent cloud cover with thick haze which only started to break up after about 11pm, allowing a lone Heinkel from III./KG 55 to dive down to an altitude of 4,000ft from where its crew to reported that there was a very large fire in the target area. Because of the poor visibility at the beginning of the action, bombing was mainly by 'Dead Reckoning' and Knickebein, but by 2am the weather had improved sufficiently to allow bombs to be

A ship in the Royal Edward Dock, Avonmouth, during World War Two. *(NFS)*

dropped visually through breaks in the cloud, although by then dense smoke was covering the Avonmouth area. Nevertheless, a total of 126 aircraft did report over Avonmouth, and 15 over Bristol, the crews of which later claimed to have dropped some 158.2 tonnes of high explosives and 54,864 incendiaries between 7.30pm and 5.08am. Losses were again small with only two aircraft being lost, 6N+CL, a Heinkel 111 from KGr 100 and L1+LK a Junkers 88 operated by I./LG 1, both of which appear to have crashed into the sea on their return flights, probably as a result of combat damage.

During the night an 'Operation Layers' was flown over Bristol by 12 Hurricanes from No.87 Squadron at Charmy Down, as well as 'Bristol's Own' No.501 Squadron back at Filton since mid-December. In spite of this results were disappointing, and to add to the problems although the local, heavy sites expended some 2,943 rounds, the absence of anti-aircraft gun fire while the fighters were patrolling over the city caused widespread comment and discontent among the long-suffering Bristolians. The Avonmouth balloon barrage also had a particularly bad night, a high explosive bomb scoring a direct hit on one of No.927 Squadron's sites causing the death of three balloon operators, and injuring seven others. On a more positive note, 28 high-explosive bombs which might otherwise have fallen on populated areas were attracted by the Chew Magna 'Starfish' decoy site. Early in the raid numerous incendiaries were released over the dock area and a number of fires were started, but with the assistance of military personnel they were once again speedily extinguished, and damage to vital buildings was confined to small dimensions. A further shower fell in the early hours of 17 January but on this occasion the fires started quickly got out of control, and damage done to docks' property and industrial buildings in the area was considerable.

Unknown to the Luftwaffe they had in fact succeeded in causing such serious damage to their objective that 17 January was the only day during the entire war, that, due to enemy action,

Avonmouth Docks were prevented from working normally. Mercifully, casualties were much fewer than in previous large-scale attacks, with only 18 people being killed and 109 injured in the whole of the Bristol area. More positive news came shortly after when No.853 Company RE reported that since the 'Blitz' began in November the unit had attended approximately 500 unexploded bomb incidents, most of these in the Bristol area, with the greatest concentration within the city boundary, where not one bomb had been blown up in situ, all being removed safely to the bomb cemetery across the River Avon in Ashton Park. This was a considerable achievement, especially as the unit had only been engaged on this hazardous work for three months!

The Changing Face of the ARP and Home Guard

As the raids became a regular part of life in Bristol, each night increasing numbers of people were taking refuge in basements and church crypts, as well as in unofficial shelters established in tunnels and caves. This caused some headaches for the civic authorities as it was clearly evident that the rather haphazard voluntary staffing arrangements then in place could no longer meet the need, so during the winter of 1940–41 they formed the Shelter Marshals' Service, which was attached to the City Engineer's department and placed under the general direction of the ARP Shelter Management Committee. A Chief Marshal was appointed, and under him Divisional and Group Marshals supervised the Shelter Marshals, each of which was responsible for about 500 people. Altogether this service went on to have some 3,000 units in its care at any one time, there were never more than 50 full-time and under 800 part-time Shelter Marshals employed. As it was intended to keep the service distinct from the Wardens', to begin with Bristol preferred the term 'Marshal', although the Ministry of Home Security did not agree and the term 'Warden' later came into general use. Those recruited were expected to discharge a wide variety of duties for not only had they to see to the cleansing of their shelters, they were also required to keep discipline, prohibit alcoholic drink of any sort, and to disperse people from the entrance where they were invariably prone to congregate. They also had to be on their guard against pilfering, to put down rowdyism, to notify the authorities about the presence of undesirable or verminous people, and to call in medical aid in cases of emergency.

Although since September 1940 it had been mandatory for Fire Watchers to be present in buildings at all times to detect fire and summon assistance, this applied only to large business premises. Consequently, in central Bristol most firms were still locked at night with keyholders many miles away, and it was only after the devastating incendiary bomb attacks of November and December that, on the last day of the year, the Minister of Home Security made an appeal to the nation to form voluntary street fire parties in every locality. To this there was an immediate response and in

MINISTRY OF HEALTH SAYS –

COUGHS AND SNEEZES SPREAD DISEASES –

trap the germs in your handkerchief

HELP TO KEEP THE NATION FIGHTING FIT

Beat
'FIREBOMB
FRITZ'

**BRITAIN
SHALL NOT
BURN**

BRITAIN'S FIRE GUARD IS BRITAIN'S DEFENCE

Bristol 65,000 members were soon recruited, distributed in some 2,900 street parties. Few records survive, but typical of these must have been the Avon Vale Fire Fighters, formed on 2 February 1941 to protect properties at the western end of Avonvale Road, in Barton Hill. Comprising 23 volunteers, their initial equipment included six stirrup pumps, nine rakes, four incendiary bomb shovels, three ladders, two spades and two 100ft hoses! Nevertheless, these ad hoc organisations did a excellent job until, in August 1941, they were superseded by the Bristol Fire Guards, established within the Civil Defence Warden's Service.

At the beginning of February, Home Guard battalions all over the country underwent yet another change of identity when they became affiliated to their respective county regiments, with the result that in the Bristol area the existing six formations were re-designated respectively, the 9th to 14th Gloucestershire (City of Bristol) Battalions, Home Guard. Each of these was now provided with the normal complement of officers who were gazetted to Home Guard commissions, and locally during the next couple of years the organisation expanded following the formation of three more battalions and the Bristol Omnibus Company's 2136 Bristol (Independent) Motor Coach Platoon. The Home Guard also provided the

personnel for a Heavy Anti-Aircraft Battery and four AA Rocket Batteries, both attached to Anti-Aircraft Command, and at its peak the organisation could boast 13,500 members of all ranks serving in the Bristol area. By early 1941 many of the Army's losses at Dunkirk had been made up and most of the Home Guard were wearing battledress, complete with stiff leather gaiters, leather belt, gas cape and helmet, and were armed not only with American and Canadian 0.300 calibre rifles, but also with

Jim Facey with a camera in his hand and a cigarette in his mouth wanders among a parade of the 7th Somerset. (Long Ashton) Battalion, Home Guard. *(Jim Facey)*

Browning Light Automatic Rifles, old Lewis guns and various grenades. Quantity and quality, however, remained a problem. As well as undertaking their normal duties, during the heavy air raids Bristol's Home Guard battalions also rendered very valuable service to the civil authorities, for which they received commendation from the Regional Commissioner, the units having assisted in directing traffic and fighting fires, acted as guides to fire-brigades brought in from outside the city, and taken part in rescue work and the removal of casualties.

Evacuate the Children

Although the heavy raids on Bristol in late 1940 should have prompted the Ministry of Health to immediately authorise a general evacuation of the city's women and children, because of official hesitation this did not even begin until May 1941. Deeply angered by this lack of action the Chairman of the Education Committee, Alderman Cox, immediately began demanding that at least school children from the most badly affected areas should be removed to places of safety. Fortunately the Regional Commissioner also supported the idea, and following a joint deputation of the city's Emergency, Education, and Health Committees, on 25 January 1941 the Minister of Health finally agreed to evacuate those living in Central and South Bristol, Avonmouth and Shirehampton. Reception areas were quickly found and on 18 February the first of some 6,370 elementary school children were sent to families in Devon and Cornwall. Parties from other parts of the city by then classified as evacuation districts followed in April and May, including 6,671 who went privately, so that between February 1941 and March 1942 at least 20,000 school children of all ages had left Bristol. Unfortunately, by the time the last evacuees were leaving around 10,000 had already drifted back, a situation which caused considerable concern for the local Emergency Committee as the raids were still expected to resume. Perhaps among them was the little girl who the *Bristol Evening World* reported had written a letter to her mother in which she grumbled; 'It's so dull, mummy – no bombs, and no sirens!'

More Pirates on the Horizon

During the third week of January 1941 extremely poor weather had again set in and many grass airfields on the Continent became waterlogged, severely hampering Luftwaffe offensive operations and ensuring that for the next month the only significant missions carried out were those flown against Swansea, Southampton and London. The situation did, however, permit a number of 'Pirate' raids on aircraft manufacturing plants to be undertaken by low flying aircraft taking advantage of the overcast conditions, and these became a regular feature of operations towards the end of the month. Locally, the first such mission was attempted on the afternoon of 22 February when the crew of a Heinkel 111 from II./KG 27 were briefed to attack the Parnall Aircraft factory at Yate, and to begin with all went well with 1G+GM successfully penetrating the defences as far as the Severn Estuary. Here the situation changed dramatically and at 2.12pm, while flying at 600ft near Avonmouth, eight rounds were loosed off at it by the 236 Battery, 76th HAA Regiment, operating the Gordano site, these exploding near the raider causing it to reduce altitude, strike a nearby barrage balloon cable, and crash on the water's edge at Portbury Wharf. This was the second, and last, enemy aircraft to be

Alderman T.H.J. Underdown, the Lord Mayor of Bristol, waves goodbye to the first school children to be evacuated from the city. *(BUP)*

brought down by Bristol's heavy anti-aircraft guns during World War Two and from it there was only one survivor, the pilot, who was detained by gunners from the Portishead site after he baled out and landed in the thick mud.

Not put off by this, another crew from II./KG 27 returned on the afternoon of 27 February when a particularly successful raid was finally made on the Parnall plant by a Heinkel 111 commanded by Oberleutnant Hermann Lohmann. Weather conditions again favoured 'Pirate' operations with much low cloud and occasional rain and drizzle in the target area, the actual attack being carried out from an altitude of less than 100ft, with seven 250kg high explosives, a number of which were fitted with delayed action fuzes. Lohmann later reported that he had come in from the north, dropping his bombs at 2.36pm along the whole length of the works, where five hits were observed on a workshop and an explosion seen in the northern part of the target area. In reality the raider had been very lucky to escape, as it had been engaged by the Yate defences, the men of the newly arrived 36th LAA Regiment having fired eight rounds of 40mm Bofors, and 40 rounds from light machine guns, scoring 15 hits and knocking out the Heinkel's port engine. Despite this, 1G+CC did manage to slowly limp back to its home airfield at Bourges, and this was the nearest

The wreckage of Heinkel He 111, 1G+GM of 4./KG 27, lies in the mud at Portbury Wharf having been shot down by anti-aircraft fire on the afternoon of 22 February 1941. The only survivor was the pilot, Leutnant Bernt Rusche, who successfully baled-out. Of the other four crewmen, the bodies of Feldwebel Georg Jankowaik, the wireless operator, and Gefreiter Erich Steinback, the gunner, have never been found, while Unteroffizier Heinrich de Wall, the flight engineer, and Feldwebel Albert Ranke, the observer, are both buried in Greenbank Cemetery. *(BUP)*

Greenbank Cemetery. The graves of Feldwebel Alfred Hanke and Unteroffizier Heinrich de Wall, who were killed when their Heinkel He 111 crashed on Portbury Wharf on 22 February 1941. *(Author's Collection)*

that the local light anti-aircraft guns ever came to bringing down an enemy aircraft during the course of World War Two. Back at Yate, considerable damage had in fact been caused, particularly to the main office block and Turret Shop, and tragically 53 workers had died, with a further 150 being injured, many of them victims of the delayed-action bomb which exploded some 10 minutes after crashing through the roof of the Drawing Office.

The 'Pirate' attacks against aircraft factories and other associated industrial installations continued into the following month, and on 6 March it was the turn of the Bristol Aeroplane Company to be targeted by a lone Heinkel from I./KG 27 commanded by Oberleutnant Hollinde. The bomber's arrival caused the Bristol sirens to sound just after 6pm on that gloomy evening, and after machine gunning streets on the outskirts of the city, seven high explosives were aimed at the Filton works. Luckily all of these missed the factory completely, but this did not stop the German crew claiming that serious damage had been caused to the objective, and for this 'achievement' they were given a special mention in the High Command of the Armed Forces communiqué issued the following day. In complete contrast, the Yate plant of Parnall Aircraft was successfully attacked for the second time by Oberleutnant Lohmann on the afternoon of 7 March, the repaired Heinkel 1G+CC dropping a further seven 250kg bombs on the works from a height of just 80ft, enabling the crew to report that at 2.05pm five bombs had made hits on assembly shops, with the other two falling on accommodation blocks and outbuildings in the southern part of the factory complex. For their actions during this and the previous attack, Lohmann and his men were also given a special mention in a high

Damage to the Parnall Aircraft plant at Yate following the 'Pirate' attacks of 27 February and 7 March 1941. (Creda)

In St Mary's churchyard at Yate can be found this memorial: 'In memory of all employees of Parnall Aircraft Ltd who lost their lives in the war as a result of air raids on the company's premises at Yate'. *(Author's Collection)*

command communiqué, and although on this occasion only three workers were killed and 20 injured, the additional damage sustained at the works caused production to come to a complete standstill while the total dispersal of the factory was undertaken.

Gloomy Mutterings in the City

During their second visit to Bristol, which took place on 3 March 1941, the Mass Observation 'blitz investigators' found the locals still grumbling about the lack of credit being given for their hardships, as well as the fact that it seemed they alone in Britain were suffering and that nobody else seemed to care. 'It seems', said their report that, 'there is always a tendency for a blitzed town to feel that its disaster is a purely local and largely personal affair.' Bristolians were also blaming Lord Beaverbrook for Bristol's recent heavy raids, because in the *Daily Express* he had compared Bristol in size and status to a similar German town bombed by the RAF, and this they considered had caused the Luftwaffe to take reprisals against the city. On a brighter note, the investigators did find that the visit of King George VI on 16 December had been of great value, because it makes the town feel that their suffering was linked, through the king, to the whole nation. In conclusion they noted,

'we should say that morale in Bristol is being left to drift in its own direction far too much, and that there is a dangerous lack of imaginative leadership and especially a rather poor

On 16 December 1940 King George IV visited Bristol. Accompanied by Alderman T.H.J. Underdown, the Lord Mayor, he is introduced to an ARP worker outside the ruins of Woolworth's store in Wine Street. *(BUP)*

quality of local leadership in this area. It would seem quite possible that depression and defeatist feelings which at present only exist in embryo might heavily and quite rapidly increase in Bristol unless something is done to give the people positive feelings of pride and purpose.'

Although the newspapers were unable to mention it, the opinion of the average Bristolian about the management of the war was that local government was slow, conservative, and too ready to listen to the advice of the wealthier inhabitants, while Mass Observation overheard a housewife remark that 'You can trust Bristol, if anyone is going to be slack and make a mess of things, it will be Bristol'. Unfortunately, by early March trekking out into the countryside each night, as well as temporary personal evacuation, had both become common, and this became something of a sore point for those who stayed put. These people, they said, left others to do the Fire Watching and their attitude was 'let their blasted houses burn'. Today it is practically impossible to ascertain just how widespread trekking from Bristol was, but in some areas of the city it was estimated that between 4 per cent and 10 per cent of the population moved out each night, while among those who stayed behind Mass Observation found that by the early spring the irregular and sporadic nature of the raiding was having a decidedly disturbing effect, with people becoming physically exhausted. Nevertheless, there was a positive side, and following a considerable effort by the Regional Information Office to inform and amuse the blitzed stayers, the meetings and concerts which had been organised were found to have been, 'received very favourably'. Bristol's night-life also improved in the late winter period, and although the city's cinemas had been in poor shape before Christmas, during February they had operated fairly normally.

CHAPTER 7

THE END OF THE STORM

March to April 1941

As 1941 progressed more equipment became available to Anti-Aircraft Command, so that during the first half of March it was possible to enlarge Bristol's heavy gun layout by the deployment of an extra eight 3" semi-mobile and twenty 3.7" mobile guns on the existing sites at Almondsbury, Avonmouth, Hambrook, Henbury, as well as on new positions at Blackboy Hill, Ashton Park, and Failand. This was to prove a timely move, for as the weather improved the Luftwaffe resumed the battle with new offensive blows against Cardiff, London, Portsmouth, Birmingham, Liverpool, Glasgow, Hull and Sheffield taking place by the middle of the month, while following the arrival of replacement aircraft and crews, by the middle of the month the German bomber force facing Britain was back to the size it had been at the end of 1940.

The Most Costly Raid of All

The Luftwaffe's attacks on Britain continued for the rest of the moonlight period in mid-March, and on 16 March the harbour installations at Bristol and Avonmouth were again selected as targets. That night of 184 crews dispatched by Luftflotte 3 some 164 subsequently reported over the area, claiming to have dropped a total of 164.25 tonnes of high explosives and 33,840 incendiaries between 8.35pm and 3.25am. To aid the pathfinders' navigation both X and Y-Verfahren operated, while the concentration point for those briefed for Bristol was centred on the Floating Harbour down-stream of the Bathurst Basin, and for those bound for Avonmouth a rectangle covering the port area, along with its adjacent warehouses and industrial works. The attackers, 108 of which were briefed to bomb Avonmouth and 76 Bristol, were drawn from I. and II./KG 1, III./KG 26, I. and II./KG 27, I.,II. and III./KG 51, I./KG 54, Stab, I., III. and III./KG 55, II./KG 76, I. and II./KG 77, and KGr 100, and although it had been intended that the bomber units of Luftflotte 2 should also participate in the raid, fog over their bases in the Low Countries, prevented them from operating. The enemy subsequently made landfall on a wide front between Axminster and Dungeness, most aircraft not flying directly to their objectives, but instead to the Cardiff area and to the east of Bristol, before running in to make their attacks.

Over the target areas the German crews initially encountered thick cloud, with mist later, and consequently bombing was predominantly by Knickebein and 'Dead Reckoning'. However, towards the close of the attack intermittent improvements in conditions enabled some crews to bomb visually, but many used searchlight activity as an indication that they were over the city, sometimes additionally aided by the glow of fires seen through cloud or mist. A large detonation followed by a tongue of flame some 3,000ft high was observed a little after midnight, and this the crews correctly assumed was the explosion of a gas holder, although they thought it to be at the St Philip's Gas Works, rather than at its true location at Stapleton Road.

Newfoundland Road, St Agnes, following the raid of 16 March. *(Jim Facey)*

This doll's house survived among the wreckage of Newfoundland Road following the raid of 16 March. *(Jim Facey)*

During the course of the raid Bristol's heavy guns fired a total of 2,370 rounds, but as the weather was so poor only nine fighters were able to operate. In spite of this the crew of a Beaufighter from No.604 Squadron did claim to have damaged a Heinkel 111 over Dorset, while of the two of the city's 'Starfish' sites which were ignited, Downside collected 74 high explosives and about 1,500 incendiaries. The local bomb disposal company also had a busy time and of the 102 suspect devices reported, 51 were confirmed, including five delayed action weapons. In spite of the inability of the local defences to do much to prevent the bombing, German casualties on 16 March were higher than in previous attempts against the Bristol area, although the majority of the six aircraft lost either ran out of fuel or crashed due to mechanical problems. Of these, five Junkers 88s crashed in France, one each from II./KG 1 and I./KG 51, and three from II./KG 76, while 9K+AK of I./KG 51 suffered a double engine failure and was forced landed at RAF Chilmark, near Dinton in Wiltshire, where the crew was subsequently taken into captivity.

Although bombs had come down in many parts of Bristol, resulting in the death of 257 people and injury to an further 391, the main attack was roughly east to west of a line from Stapleton Road Station, through the city centre to Clifton Down Station, while in addition to the central area itself the districts most seriously affected were Fishponds, Eastville, Whitehall, Easton, St Paul's, Montpelier, Kingsdown, Cotham, Redland and Clifton. Of all the air attacks carried out against Bristol this was perhaps the worst as due to the poor visibility over the target area the raid had drifted into the 'working class' suburbs of East Bristol, to which a number of bombers had been attracted by a few large fires that had developed in the Easton area. This went some of the way towards explaining why the city's casualty figures were higher than at any time during the war, the other main cause being the premature 'All Clear' which was sounded at 1.40am. As a consequence of this some people who had just left the relative safety of their shelters were caught by bombs dropped by the first of the 29 Junkers 88s from II./KG 76, aircraft ordered to undertake the final phase of the raid, and no official explanation was ever forthcoming as to why it took so long for the city's sirens to once again wail out their warning.

As the attack had been so damaging ARP reinforcements had to be moved into Bristol from Clevedon, Warmley, Gloucestershire, Somerset, Bath, and Wiltshire, while some 35 Fire Brigades from Gloucestershire, Somerset, Wiltshire, Dorset and Devon also arrived to assist the local fire fighters. From the moment the Germans started attacking, the Civil Defence and Police Services became particularly vulnerable as they often had to operate in the open while bombs were still falling. Nevertheless, on this occasion the final casualties count revealed more than might normally have been expected, some 40 personnel having made the supreme sacrifice. Of these, 20 were Fire Watchers, six Fire Guards, four Shelter Wardens, three ARP Wardens, two Rescue Service members and two War Reserve Constables, but also included in their number were people as diverse as a Decontamination Party member, a Casualty Service Auxiliary Nurse and a Report & Control Service Liaison Officer.

Yet again Bill Hares was in a good position to record the night's events and in his diary wrote:

'Planes over. Flares, incendiaries, and bombs begin falling almost immediately. Big fire started at Lawrence Hill Bus Depot. Planes are coming in continuously. Seems that we're in

Victims of German bombs covered by sheets in a road in Easton following the raid of 16 March. *(Jim Facey)*

for another picnic. Wonder what the night will bring forth. The Huns are certainly mixing them well tonight. Not much chance of their missing the town with the fires they have started so early. Nothing happening just around us, so we go to the top floor to see what and where things are occurring. Two or three fires burning to the east and smoke and flame begins to pour from Anderson's Rubber Factory in Stokes Croft. The blue incandescent light of exploding incendiaries can be seen in several different directions, and bunches of chandelier flares are being continually dropped.'

'Ground defences are firing tracer shells. Barrage over-head provides suitable 'incidental music', interrupted by the scream of high explosives. We get tired of ducking and just anticipate where they are likely to fall. I watch a string of incendiaries bursting as they strike the roofs of Ellbroad Street. They seem to be coming straight for the factory, and then take a sudden turn across the ruins of Castle Street, where they are quite harmless. Another lot falls straight up Philadelphia Street – explosive incendiaries, this time – and these are followed by a stick of H.E.'s which pass right over the buildings and fall with tremendous explosions in City and Ashley Roads. Anderson's and the buildings around are now a huge burning mass, but still the Hun has not had enough. A plane comes in very low right over Kingsdown and Stokes Croft, lets go both heavy explosive and incendiaries. It seems that the

A double decker bus blown on its side in Easton Road, just outside the entrance to Lawrence Hill bus depot following the raid of 16 March. *(Jim Facey)*

Easton Road during the 1990s showing the Pit Pony public house on the left and the entrance to Lawrence Hill bus garage on the right. *(Author's Collection)*

blast of the bombs temporarily smothered the fire. Planes are easing off now. Gunfire only spasmodic. A lull ensues, and the "All Clear" sounds.'

'Another siren wails. Surely Jerry has had enough for one night! But no. The fires he previously started guide him, but this time the bombs seem to be aimed at residential areas. It goes on hour after hour, until you are sickened utterly by the futility and continued hopelessness of it all. You no longer pay any heed when a stick of bombs falls quite near. In fact, I was surprised to see the explosion of a big 'un before the whistle of it had ceased. Though I've been through several blitzes and bombs have fallen all around, this is the first time I have actually seen the eruption of flames and debris. It left me with a very queer and helpless feeling. The "All Clear" sounded, and another memorable night has been safely passed through.'

Two Very Courageous Ladies

Shortly after the initial 'Alert' had sounded a bomb partially demolished a house in Alfred Place, Kingsdown, leaving it in a very dangerous state, with gas escaping from a fractured pipe. Frank Braund, his wife Lilian, their three children Jean, Shirley and Valery, as well as Mrs Braund's sister and her mother were all in the basement when the bomb landed, and although Mr Braund and the baby Valery were killed, all the others were alive but entombed under a great deal of wreckage. To add to the problems Mrs Braund, who was trapped by the legs, was also in an advanced state of pregnancy. When the call for assistance was received at the Bristol Maternity Hospital, Assistant Matron Stevens and Sister Frampton immediately volunteered to attend the incident even though the raid was at its height with bombs falling all around the area. Although conditions were so bad that it was practically impossible to continue with the rescue operation Elsie Stevens insisted on being lowered through a narrow opening and, by lying flat, was able to reach one of the victims. Although her difficulties were further compounded by the fact that the only light available was that given by a torch, with the assistance of her colleague and the Rescue Party, the old lady and two children were released and passed through a grating to safety.

As the pregnant Mrs Braund was found to be completely buried under debris, Violet Frampton went back to the hospital to obtain morphia and, when she returned, Assistant Matron Stevens was again lowered into the cellar in order to give the patient an injection. By that time conditions were so dangerous that rescue work overhead had to be suspended as there was the grave risk of the whole

A rescue squad at work on St Michael's Hill. *(Jim Facey)*

building collapsing owing to blast and the shaking of the debris. Despite this, and in an atmosphere made poisonous by the escaping gas, the two courageous ladies again went down to their patient, and by 3am had managed to release her head. They were then able to make her more comfortable, sustaining her with sips of warm tea, and although still pinned down by the legs she managed to stay cheerful throughout her ordeal. Right through the night they remained with her while the Rescue Party worked to clear a way out, but at about 8 o'clock in the morning it was thought necessary to call in a doctor who immediately went down into the

The wreckage of 1 Alfred Place, Kingsdown, following the raid of 16 March. It was here that Assistant Matron Stevens and Sister Frampton each won the George Medal.

cellar to join the ladies from the Maternity Hospital. All three then remained with Mrs Braund in the most awkward and dangerous of circumstances until she was finally released in the early afternoon, and taken away to hospital. For this amazing devotion to duty, outstanding bravery and complete disregard for their own safety, on 30 May 1941 Assistant Matron Elsie Lilian Stevens and Sister Violet Eva Alice Frampton were each awarded the George Medal.

The Turning Point at Last

Once again a serious raid on Bristol prompted a reinforcement of the area's air defence, and on 26 March three 3.7" mobile anti-aircraft guns were put in place at the new Rodway site, the same day on which Colerne airfield received its first operational unit, No. 307 (Polish) Squadron operating single-engined Boulton Paul Defiant night fighters equipped with a turret containing four machine guns. Although in the latter part of March the return of poor weather again severely restricted German operations, attacks were made on Hull, London and Plymouth, culminating in an attempt against harbour installations in the Bristol area on the night of 29 March. This was made possible by a slight improvement in conditions which occurred late in the day over some bomber bases in North West France, permitting a limited strike to be directed at Bristol by the Junkers 88s from III./KG 1 and II./KG 76, and Avonmouth by the Heinkels from KGr 100 and III./KG 26. The objectives at Avonmouth were the harbour and industrial installations, while at Bristol the concentration point was between the east end of the Floating Harbour and the two gasholders at Canon's Marsh, and to

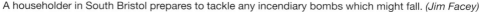

A householder in South Bristol prepares to tackle any incendiary bombs which might fall. *(Jim Facey)*

assist the Heinkels in locating the targets both X and Y-Verfahren was in use, the crews of III./KG 26 later reporting that the Y Beam signal was well received.

The raiders crossed the French coast near Morlaix and Brest, and later in the vicinity of Dieppe, before coming in over Lyme Bay and approaching their objectives from the south-south-east. Although the majority of the aircraft passed just east of the Bristol area, the run-up to the target was made from all directions, with some of the aircraft flying as far west as the Welsh coast before circling to deliver their attacks from the north or north-west. The overcast conditions in the West Country ensured that no night fighters were operational, and although Bristol's heavy anti-aircraft guns fired 900 rounds at the raiders, no German aircraft were lost, or even damaged, during the operation. So it was that from the force of 38 aircraft dispatched, some 35 subsequently claimed to have dropped a total 33 tonnes of high explosives and 13,088 incendiaries in the harbour areas of Bristol and Avonmouth between 9.05 and 10.08pm.

Over Bristol the cloud and mist was responsible for the fact that only five crews reported that they had bombed visually, the other 15 using 'Dead Reckoning' and Knickebein, while in spite of the fires started at Avonmouth helping to guide the following four crews who were unable to use X-Verfahren, they still experienced difficulty in locating their objectives. However, this lack of visibility in the target area ensured that no incidents were reported in Bristol itself all the aircraft, either knowingly or not, attacking Avonmouth or dropping their bombs in rural localities across the southern part of Gloucestershire, and this ensured that the local casualty figures amounted to only six people killed and 17 injured.

Nevertheless, in Avonmouth Docks where a number of fires were started, three tanks belonging to the Anglo-American Oil Company burned so furiously that it was not possible to extinguish the last of them until late the following afternoon, but not before foam tenders and personnel from some 20 fire brigades from Gloucestershire, Somerset, Wiltshire, Dorset, Berkshire, Worcestershire, Herefordshire, Buckinghamshire, Oxfordshire, the Birmingham area, and London had been drafted in to assist. As well as destroying valuable oil stocks, this fire was to have unfortunate consequences for Superintendent Albert Maunder, Bristol Fire Brigade's senior officer, who resigned on 30 April following criticism of his handling of the incident.

Fortunately for the long-suffering inhabitants of Bristol, the Luftwaffe's bomber force facing them was not to maintain its new found strength for long, as not only had Luftflotte 3 lost KGr 606 in mid-January, when it began exchanging its old Do 17s for Ju 88s, but in late March orders were also issued transferring to the whole of KG 51 to the Balkans, a movement which marked the start of the steady decline in the Germans offensive capability in the West. By this time a turning point had also been reached regarding the RAF's night fighting ability, and from then on Luftwaffe losses during nocturnal raids steadily mounted, mainly as a result of the expansion of the GCI system. During April and May No.604 Squadron at Middle Wallop, which went on to become the highest-scoring night fighter formation in the RAF, claimed 30 raiders destroyed, including three Heinkel 111s engaged in raids on Bristol. Other units were soon following their example and No.600, a Beaufighter squadron which did not arrive at Colerne until 27 April, went on to shoot down a Junkers 88 and a Heinkel 111 before the end of the month, as well as two more Heinkels in early May.

The night sky over
Ashton Gate lit up by
anti-aircraft tracers and
searchlight beams during
an air raid. *(Jim Facey)*

The weather over the Continent now improved, and normal Luftwaffe operations finally re-started after nightfall on 3 April, when an attempt was made against the harbour and industrial installations at Avonmouth by a force of 94 aircraft from Luftflotte 3. Of these, the leading aircraft approached from the Dieppe and Le Havre area, before crossing the English coast over Poole Bay, while the remainder routed via Brittany and Lyme Bay. The majority of the attackers then spread out before reaching Bristol, and consequently the run-up to Avonmouth was made from many different directions. As there was still considerable cloud cover over the port only a relatively small number of crews were able to bomb visually, others being forced to switch their efforts to Bristol, the alternative target.

In their final report the Germans claimed that 31 Heinkel 111s from III./KG 26, II./KG 27 and KGr 100 and the 45 Junkers 88s from II. and III./KG 1, I. and II./KG 54, II./KG 76 and KGr 806 had reached the Bristol area, and to guide the pathfinders both X and Y-Verfahren were operating, some four crews from III./KG 26 successfully using the Y Beam. At the beginning of the attack there was 70 per cent cloud cover which cleared to 20 per cent with a half moon between 11pm and midnight, but thereafter conditions deteriorated and rain set in, the target area soon becoming completely covered in cloud. Consequently only 49 aircraft actually reported over Avonmouth, and although some crews bombed visually, the majority used 'Dead Reckoning' and Knickebein, while the remaining 27 aircraft attacked the Floating Harbour and industrial area of

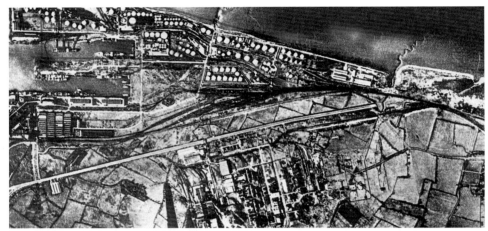

Bristol-Avonmouth, harbour installations, target GB 45 55 with 45 54. Document b3, one vertical and one oblique photograph, issued May 1941.

Bristol where the bombing was entirely by 'Dead Reckoning' and radio methods. Returning crews reported dropping some 79.8 tonnes of high explosives and 8,938 incendiaries over Bristol and Avonmouth between 9.16pm and 0.45am, but as a result of the poor visibility over the target only moderate success was claimed for the operation.

Although the weather had done much to prevent fire development during the raid the local fire fighters, reinforced by 48 brigades from various parts of Gloucestershire, Somerset, Devon and Wiltshire, were so prompt and effective that although nearly 9,000 incendiaries had been dropped on Bristol, particularly between St Michael's Hill and Redland Green, only 37 minor fires were recorded, all having being extinguished by the time the last raiders were leaving the area. With inadequate target marking having taken place, when the High Explosive attack developed it was on a line between the Horseshoe Bend and Filton, ensuring that in Avonmouth only a few scattered incidents were reported, while in the whole of the Bristol area only 22 people lost their lives with a further 56 sustaining some degree of injury.

During the night RAF Fighter Command's No.10 Group flew some 15 defensive sorties, and during one of these a Beaufighter from No.604 Squadron, flown by the legendary Flight Lieutenant John Cunningham with Sergeant C.F. 'Jimmy' Rawnsley as his AI Operator, shot down V4+AR of III./KG 1, the Ju 88A-5 subsequently crashing into the sea south of the Isle of Wight, the only loss sustained by the attack force. On the ground the Downside 'Starfish' site drew 25 High Explosives, while Bristol's heavy guns fired a total of 3327 rounds in spite of five small bombs falling across the Gordano site operated by 236 Battery, 76th HAA Regiment. One bomb hit a hut, killing one man

Damage to modern semi-detached houses in Cheriton Place, Westbury on Trym, caused by the raid of 3 April. *(Jim Facey)*

and injuring five others, while others were responsible for destroying a height finder and damaging two guns and some ancillary equipment.

The Germans followed up this attack the following night with 105 aircraft taking off once more to raid the harbour and industrial installations at Avonmouth. Of these 38 Heinkel 111s from III./KG 26, II./KG 27 and KGr 100 and 50 Junkers 88s of I. and II./KG 54, I., II. and III./KG 77 and KGr 806 subsequently claimed to have attacked the objective between 9.15pm and 1.30am, with 80.4 tonnes of high explosives and 19,675 incendiaries, while two Junkers 88s, both from KG 77, reported dropping two tonnes of high explosives and 468 incendiaries on South-East Bristol as an alternative target. On this occasion the attackers crossed the French coast at a number of points in the vicinity of Berck-Plage, Dieppe, Le Havre, Cherbourg and Morlaix, before crossing the Channel and coming in on a wide front between Beachy Head and Lyme Regis. The electronic beams were set up over the area in exactly the same manner in which they had

Switch off that LIGHT!

LESS LIGHT – MORE PLANES

been on the previous night, and although the crews of KGr 100 and III./KG 26 successfully operated with X and Y-Verfahren, the latter Gruppe were unlucky enough to have a Heinkel 111 brought down while on its run-in to the target, the stricken bomber eventually crashing at Hewish, near Weston-super-Mare, the gunner and wireless operator both losing their lives. Although this was another victory for a Beaufighter from No.604 Squadron, on this occasion crewed by Flying Officer Edward Crew and Sergeant Norman Guthrie, the other 27 defensive sorties flown during night by RAF Fighter Command's No.10 Group met with no success, and consequently in spite of the fact that 1H+ED was the only German aircraft that failed to return from Avonmouth, on account of its crew's specialist abilities, it was a significant victory for the defenders.

As the Beaufighter pilot subsequently pointed out in his combat report, to begin with it was a fine clear night with a half moon, although visibility did deteriorate slightly during the latter part of the operation. Not surprisingly, the participating crews subsequently reported that the target area

Bristol-Avonmouth, Zinc Works of the Imperial Smelting Corp. Ltd, target GB 71 1. Document c, the plan, and issued 17 October 1938.

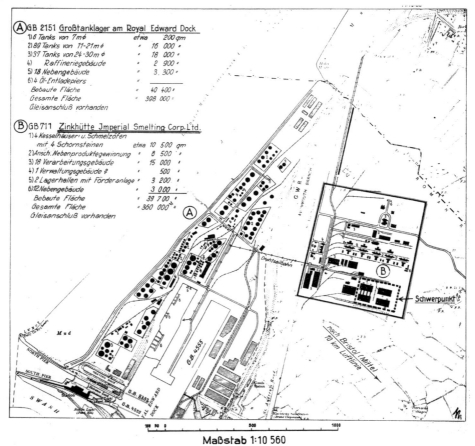

Maßstab 1:10 560

was visible for much of the attack, and at times was very clearly seen in the moonlight, therefore bombing was predominantly visual, with only a small proportion of crews finding it necessary to resort to either 'Dead Reckoning' or Knickebein. At the start of the operation the whole of Bristol was lit up by a large number of chandelier flares, some 15 of which were counted in the air at one time, while high explosives and incendiaries followed at regular intervals. Avonmouth was principally affected, and to a lesser extent the Westbury and Whitchurch districts, but minimal damage was in fact caused at Avonmouth Docks as many of the incendiaries which fell in the vicinity burnt out harmlessly on high ground in Shirehampton Park.

Nevertheless, the most serious incident that night occurred at the National Smelting Company, where production was seriously affected, particularly in the Fertilizer and Acid Works, but considering the scope of the raid and the number of high explosives dropped, casualties were again remarkably light, amounting to just three dead and 21 injured. The promptitude of the Street Fire Fighting Parties, together with the actions of the local firemen and the 24 reinforcing brigades sent in from Gloucestershire, Somerset, Wiltshire and Dorset, once again largely contributed to the immunity of the city from significant damage, and only one serious and 21 minor fires were started, all of which were well under control by 2am.

During the course of the night the anti-aircraft defences expended even more shells than on the previous raid with a total of 6,450 rounds being fired by Bristol's guns, but the cost was high, some three gunners losing their lives on two separate sites. One man was killed and seven injured at Purdown when a gun belonging to 238 Battery, 76th HAA Regiment, fired prematurely, while a

bomb landed on the Brickfields battery where two men from the same unit died. The 'Starfish' decoys were also in operation and Downside drew 10 high-explosive bombs which might otherwise have fallen to the north in Bristol.

Glasgow and Liverpool were the main targets on the night of 7 April, but a diversionary raid by 22 aircraft from KGr 100, I. and II./KG 54, KGr 806, I., II. and III./KG 55 was also carried out against the harbour installations at Bristol, nine of the bombers subsequently attacking

St Clement's Church at the corner of Newfoundland Road and Houlton Street after an attack by a lone Heinkel from I./KG 55 on the night of 9 April 1941. The vicar, the Revd G.R. Fooke and others can be seen digging in the rubble of the vestry. (Jim Facey)

Avonmouth as an alternative. In addition a further 11 aircraft from KGr 100, II. and III./KG 1, I. and III./KG 27 unable to locate their main targets also bombed Bristol, where nine people were injured and some serious damage caused in Horfield. As it was overcast in the target area, with total cloud at 3,200ft, bombing was carried out using only Knickebein and 'Dead Reckoning' methods, while after the raid, which lasted from 9.13 until 10.17pm and saw 29.2 tonnes of high explosives and 6,442 incendiaries dropped, all the participating crews returned safely to base.

The Last Widespread Raid

In order to counteract the increasing number of German raids, modifications to Bristol's anti-aircraft gun layout continued to be carried out, and the following day three 3.7" mobiles moved to take up position at another new site at Lodge Farm, near Portishead. Four 3.7" mobiles earmarked for the other additional site at Pilning were not deployed until the end of the month and were therefore not in place before Bristol's last large scale attack, the so called 'Good Friday Raid', took place, immediately after the Luftwaffe had visited Coventry, Birmingham and Tyneside.

The operation against Bristol carried out on the night of 11 April was undertaken by 177 aircraft, of which 138 from Luftflotte 3 and 15 from Luftflotte 2 subsequently reported over target between 10.10pm and 3.15am, the crews later claiming to have dropped 193 tonnes of high explosives and 36,888 incendiaries on the harbour and industrial installations in South West and West Central Bristol, as well as on Avonmouth and Portishead Docks. Yet again both X and Y-Verfahren were

The burning remains of John Wright's printing works on Colston Avenue following the raid of 11 April. (*Jim Facey*)

Colston Avenue as it was in the 1990s.
(Author's Collection)

operating to assist the pathfinders in locating the objectives, and that night the participating units from Luftflotte 3 were II. and III./KG 1, III./KG 26, I., II. and III./KG 27, I. and II./KG 54, Stab, I., II. and III./KG 55, KG 100 and KGr 806, assisted by Luftflotte 2's contribution, the Heinkel 111s of I. and II./KG 53.

At 9.05pm the first raiders approached flying due north over Morlaix in Brittany, and after crossing the English coast in the vicinity of Lyme Bay, reached Bristol at 9.52pm, These were quickly followed by another small group which, after crossing the Channel Islands, made landfall just east of Portland at 9.45pm. There was then something of a lull before a second phase began at 11.35pm when raiders from the direction of Ostend skirted the south coast from Beachy Head to Selsey Bill before turning north over the Isle of Wight. These were then followed by others which approached from Fécamp, before crossing the Isle of Wight, and from the direction of Caen and Point de Barfleur to come in over Portland, while a final group routed via Rennes, the Channel Islands and Lyme Bay. In the target area the weather was generally fine with a full moon and a high layer of fleecy cloud which allowed the bombing to be carried out mainly with visual reference, although, from time to time the appearance of thick cloud required the use of either 'Dead Reckoning' or radio assisted methods. At 2.10am the crews of I./KG 55 noted a large explosion followed by a flame rising nearly 5,000ft into the sky, announcing the destruction of a gas holder at Canon's Marsh, the third to be lost at Bristol during the 'blitz'. Likewise, the aircraft attacking Avonmouth also reported bombing visually, but at nearby Portishead a considerable amount of smoke was encountered.

The German attrition rate on night operations was now mounting and five bombers were lost, two Junkers 88s from III./KG 1 and II./KG 54, and three Heinkel 111s, from III./KG 26, III./KG 27, and III./KG 55. Of these, just one fell in England, 1G+HT from III./KG 27 which crashed at Lydlinch, in Dorset, at 1.35am while on its outward flight, another victim of a No.604 Squadron Beaufighter crewed by our old friends Squadron Leader John Cunningham and Sergeant C.F. 'Jimmy' Rawnsley. To combat the intruders Fighter Command had flown a total of 39 sorties which had resulted in further claims for a Heinkel shot down over Dorset by a Defiant of No.307 Squadron from Colerne, and a Junkers destroyed by Hurricane of No.87 Squadron from Charmy Down, while two other crews from No.604 Squadron reported bringing down a second Heinkel 111, as well as a lone Junkers 88. The local 'Starfish' sites were also successful, and drew a total of 34 high explosives, while in Bristol more than 100 suspect unexploded devices were reported, including more delayed action bombs than in any other raid, one of which tragically claimed the life a bomb disposal officer

A view of the corner of King Street and Welsh Back following the raid of 11 April. *(Jim Facey)*

King Street as it was in the 1990s. *(Author's Collection)*

from the local Brislington-based No.7 Bomb Disposal Squad RE. During the night the local anti-aircraft guns, including Weston-super-Mare's, also fired 6,765 rounds, although the balloon barrage around Bristol and Filton suffered fourteen balloons damaged by shrapnel, some of which undoubtedly came from exploding anti-aircraft shells!

In Bristol, ARP Control reported that the first phase of the raid began shortly after 10pm when the majority of the incidents straddled a north and south line from Bristol Bridge to Horfield. Nevertheless, although an observer posted in a vantage point overlooking the city saw the white glaring patches caused by incendiaries igniting all over the area grow and brighten, 'Within minutes it was as though someone was drawing a blanket over them, the light died down and disappeared'. This was of course due to the prompt and efficient actions of the local Street Fire Parties, who were among the quickest in the country at tackling the fire-bombs, and as a result of their sterling efforts later raiders were deprived of a valuable navigation and bombing aid.

The second phase commenced just after midnight and during this entirely different districts of the city were affected, high explosives on this occasion being scattered over the southern part of the central area, including St Augustine's, Bedminster and Knowle, while to a lesser extent, Avonmouth and Fishponds were also affected. Considerably more damage occurred during this phase and the Fire Liaison Officer subsequently reported 28 small fires, 144 medium and two serious in the Bristol area, while to further compound the difficulties the AFS Station in Jacob's Wells Road received a direct hit. To assist the city, reinforcements of fire and ARP services were moved in from surrounding areas, and during the night about 262 fire pumps were in use, ensuring that all fires were under control by 07.00 hrs.

Obviously as such a large number of aircraft had been employed casualties were heavy, some 180 people being killed and 382 injured in the Bristol area, while the Civil Defence Services suffered particularly badly with 14 Fire Guards, 12 Fire Watchers, four ARP Wardens and two members of the Casualty Service all loosing their lives. The night also proved very costly for the fire services, with two messengers and eight firemen killed, including four who were working at Wright's on Closton Avenue when a large high-explosive landed nearby, blowing their bodies a considerable

When St Philip's Bridge received a direct hit at 2.20am on 12 April 1941 it spelled the end of Bristol's last tram route by effectively cutting off the electricity supply from the Counterslip generating station. (visible in the background) to the trams which still ran out to Kingswood. *(Jim Facey)*

St Philip's Bridge as it was in the 1990s. *(Author's Collection)*

distance away. Canon J.S. Smith, an ambulance driver, later found three of them lying in the road opposite the public conveniences, all badly burned, and had the unpleasant job releasing them from the melted tarmac, in which the grisly marks remained for many years after.

For the last time Bill Hares diary entry gives us an insight into what it was like to live through a large scale air raid on Bristol:

'The siren goes and we stand by as usual. In come the planes. The barrage opens up immediately, but unlike the first blitzes, there are now plenty of Fire Watchers. Matters are more organised; the novelty of being subjected to aerial bombardment has faded, and we know our own capabilities to deal with any fire bombs that fall in the district. Unable to see much in the street we go up to the top floor to take a look if anything should happen. It's not a bad view; orange and red flares drift slowly down, the red bursts of ack-ack shells followed by the drifting white haloes light the sky while we wait for the more vigorous and devastating part of the play to begin.'

'With a terrific shriek a large bomb falls on Broadmead, a very early present! Then a string of incendiaries swishes across Cotham and beyond. We watch a series of different lines of incendiaries and applaud or criticise when they are not outed quickly or allowed to take hold. In quick succession five lots are plotted and it is now apparent that Jerry needs more than incendiaries to get the people of this town panicky. In spite of this, there are big fires raging in Cheltenham Road, Stokes Croft and Kingsdown, and it seems that Jerry is determined to increase these. My mates and I stand looking out of the windows wondering if and when anything is coming our way. It seems again we are on the edge of things and have got to be content with the role of spectators. Then, in the distance, the blue incandescent light of exploding fire bombs is seen down across the roofs and streets starting from the top of Stokes Croft, coming halfway down then taking a south-west turn towards us. We watch them come nearer; Brunswick Square, Rosemary Street and up Quaker's Friars. I shout to my mates to duck under the table, expecting to have the rest right through our own roof.'

'Seconds pass. We think it's all right now, and one of us suggests we go and look for souvenirs. Coming down the stairs we get a shock. There is our souvenir burning away in the office. Using the now successful method of past raids, I let the bomb have a full bucket of water. Up she goes in a sheet of flame and sparks. Harry comes behind with the sandbags and dumps them on top, and Bert brings up the rear with two more buckets of water. Beyond a little mess no damage is done. We now go down to the street to see if any more had dropped near. What a difference from the first blitzes when a single fire bomb could do tremendous damage through the lack of training and knowledge! The All Clear goes, and we prepare for a night's rest.'

'But we have no luck. Off goes "Moaning Minnie" again, and we get ready for the second half of the show. The barrage, which, had tailed off considerably during the last hour opens up again with fresh intensity, and while watching the innumerable bursts in the sky we get the surprise of our lives. The great black shapes of a couple of German bombers come sailing in well below the balloons. With three guns firing from them at the balloons and the ground defences they pass right overhead, and let their load of hate fall near the Centre. The attack now shifts to the middle of the city, and fires spring up in Redcliff Street, the Centre, and Park Street. They quickly get out of hand, and become beacons, a guide for far more terrific bombing. A few more incendiaries across Stokes Croft, St Michael's Hill, and Park Row. Big fire starts near the gasometer at the back of the Eye Hospital. Hell let loose again; terrific bomb attack. Fire in Park Street now assumes huge proportions, and flames leap high into the air, reminiscent of the first blitz. Raid goes on till early morning, by which time the early fires had died down, and I think everybody had had just about enough.'

With the 'Good Friday Raid' over, on Monday 14 April 1941 Miss M. Fagnani, who lived in Colston Street, was moved to commit to paper her thoughts on the weekend's events:

'It is a strange and awful Eastertide for Bristol, and the city is full of morbid sightseers, whom I have no time for. All the big papers on Sunday have given us a good write up; they say we have had the worst raid outside London so far, and Bristol is the worst blitzed city of the lot. So if we exist at the end of the war we shall have something to feel proud about for having "stayed put". Though I am no church-goer, I believe in God, and through it all I have never lost my faith.'

The Mass Observation 'blitz team' were also interested in Bristolians' reactions to the latest attack, and during their final visit to the city on 22 April they reported that damage remained 'the dominant topic', with approximately half of all conversations overheard being personal accounts of

Palmyra Road, Bedminster, with Avonleigh Road to the left and the back of Elmdale Road off to the right, following the raid of 11 April. *(Jim Facey)*

dangerous experiences. There was also spontaneous comment on the inadequacy of the city's shelters, as well as the need for more tunnels, some of which by that time were being improved, bricked and cemented, although to do so it had been necessary to move out some of the regular shelterers, again a source of fiercely unfavourable talk.

Unknown to the man in the street, since the spring of 1941 anti-aircraft gun layout around Bristol had also been under review, with the main object of engaging enemy aircraft further out from

the existing Gun Defended Area. To this end, early in May it was announced that two additional sites were to be built at Gaunt's Earthcott and Henfield, while the Failand position was to be moved to

Flames over Raleigh Road, Ashton Gate, early on the morning of 12 April. *(Jim Facey)*

St Francis Church, North Street, Ashton Gate, burning out on the morning of 12 April. *(Jim Facey)*

Backwell, and that at Ashton Park to Chew Stoke, thus allowing some of the previously used positions to be abandoned, and others renamed. As a result of this reorganisation, for the rest of the war 20 gun sites were maintained around the city, and were henceforth known as Portbury (Portishead renamed), Lodge Farm, Gordano (re-named Markham in June 1944), St Georges (Avonmouth renamed), Cribbs, Westbury, Rockingham, Pilning, Almondsbury, Earthcott, Brickfields, Henfield, Purdown, Rodway, Hanham, Keynsham, Whitchurch, Chew, Reservoir and Backwell.

Winston Churchill and his wife visit Bedminster 12 April 1941. Among those accompanying him are Sir Charles Maby the Chief Constable, Mr J.G. Winant the American Ambassador, and General Sir Hugh Elles the Regional Controller. *(Jim Facey)*

CHAPTER 8

THE DIMINISHING THREAT

May 1941 to December 1942

B
ack in early 1941 it had become clear to everyone that the 'blackout' regulations imposed at the start of the war had made working and travelling not just difficult, but also extremely dangerous. Therefore, in an attempt to provide people with more daylight when it was most required, on 25 February 'British Summer Time' had been introduced early, and this remained in force until 2am on 4 May 1941 when the new 'British Double Summer Time' replaced it, this being some two hours in advance of GMT. Although this daylight-saving measure ensured that it then got darker later in the evening, in the morning people still had the problem of grouping their way to work through the twilight. Nevertheless, it remained in use from then on, and when the clocks were changed in the spring and autumn they did so from BST to BDST and back until the latter was finally discontinued on 2 April 1945.

In spite of the fact that nobody in Britain would have realised at the time, the 'Good Friday Raid' had actually marked the end of the main 'Blitz on Bristol', as after that the Luftwaffe switched their

The Bristol Motor Company's premises in Winterstoke Road well alight early in the morning of 8 May. *(Jim Facey)*

Looking towards Regent Street, Clifton, the remains of Windmill & Lewis's garage in Merchants Road, following the raid of 8 May. *(Jim Facey)*

attention to targets elsewhere in Britain. This having been said, during early May German bombers did raid Bristol on a number of nights, albeit in relatively small numbers, the crews of the aircraft involved having selected the city as an alternative after finding themselves unable to locate their main objectives in the Midlands and North of England. The most serious of these raids took place on the night of 7 May when, as a result of total cloud cover over Liverpool, some 16 aircraft from II. and III./KG 27, KGr 100, I., II. and III./KG 55 attacked Bristol, causing much damage in the Knowle, Bedminster, Clifton and Central areas, killing 20 people and injuring a further 84. Among the casualties were four of No.951 Squadron's balloon operators who manned the Bristol barrage, all of whom were injured, one fatally, by a bomb which fell directly on to their site.

Although by now the majority of German bombers had moved east in preparation for the forthcoming invasion of the Soviet Union, the Luftwaffe in the West still possessed some offensive capability, and as part of the strategy of masking the withdrawal of the main bomber force the use of the minelaying units operating against England was reviewed. At the end of May this resulted in instructions being issued to permit their temporary deployment against selected land targets where they were to assist the remaining bomber Gruppen by dropping 'Land Mines', and although Bristol was not included in the list, this policy was eventually to have tragic consequences for some local people. These weapons were in fact standard 1,000kg parachute mines, of the type normally sown in important sea lanes around the coast, but which when used against land targets were fitted with impact fuses, their subsequent detonation causing considerable blast damage as the mines had very

The corner of Merchants Road, Clifton, looking up towards Clifton Down following the raid of 8 May. *(Jim Facey)*

Almorah Road, Victoria Park, looking towards Raymend Avenue, following the dropping of a land mine early on the morning of 12 June 1941. *(Jim Facey)*

thin outer cases. In spite of local Civil Defence reports often mentioning such devices during the winter of 1940–41, according to German records no 'Land Mines' were actually aimed at Bristol until in an unprecedented act of destruction just after 4am on the morning of 12 June a lone Heinkel 111 from I./KG 28 dropped two on the Bedminster area killing 16 people and injuring 77 others, one of the fatalities being a man operating the city's balloon barrage. This aircraft, unable to locate its assigned target in the Birmingham area, had again selected Bristol as a suitable alternative with devastating results for the inhabitants of the tightly packed house in Almorah Road and Willway Street.

Smoke Screens and Meacons

By mid-June 1941 the 'Air Battle for England' as German historians refer to the period since the fall of France, had at last drawn to a close as the vast majority of Luftflotte 2, together with the most of the bomber units of Luftflotte 3, had then completed their move to Eastern Germany and Poland in readiness for the attack on Russia, which opened shortly before dawn on 22 June. These massive withdrawals ensured that by August 1941 only about 120 bomber and minelaying aircraft remained to continue to enforce the blockade of Britain, but with the possibility still remaining that they would return for a second winter campaign in the West, those responsible for the air defence of the United Kingdom were still making improvements and additions to the system.

One new measure involved the use of smoke screens, something the Ministry of Home Security had begun implementing on a small scale in October 1940. It was now decided that these should be extended to provided to provide cover for as many vital targets as possible, and personnel from the Pioneer Corps were earmarked to man them. The first of these, from No.810 (SM) Company, arrived in Bristol on 25 June 1941 to operate a screen around Avonmouth Docks which was made up of an outer circuit of up to 45 mobile Haslar generators arranged on a radius of about 1,500yd around the target, plus an inner circuit formed by 2,510 No.24 Mark II static generators installed about 1,000yd out from the target, notably 5 to 10yd apart along the Portway, Portview Road and St Andrew's Road. The Pioneers did not have to wait long to test the system, it first being during a Birmingham raid early on the morning of 5 July, when a single Ju 88 from Kü. Fl. Gr. 606 which was suffering from technical problems dropped two tonnes of high explosives on Bristol, killing a young married couple in Cromwell Road, St Andrew's.

While undertaking such operations over Britain the Luftwaffe made considerable use of radio beacons located in France to assist their navigators, and even against these radio countermeasures were employed. Instead of straightforward jamming, the signal from each individual beacon was received and then re-radiated from a 'Meacon' transmitter located in Britain, thereby effectively falsifying the beacon's position. The first local success for this system early on the morning of 24 July,

Willway Street, Bedminster, looking towards East Street, following the dropping of a land mine early on the morning of 12 June 1941. *(Jim Facey)*

when the Lympshan transmitter, then re-radiating the Brest beacon, caused Junkers Ju 88 4D+DL from I./KG 30, which had been on a mission to Birkenhead Docks, to land undamaged at RAF Broadfield Down, an airfield which at that time was still under construction. Low on fuel and thinking they were over France, the crew put down at 6.20am on the first aerodrome they saw, Unteroffizier Wolfgang Hosie in fact making the first landing on what is now the main runway of Bristol International Airport! The Junkers subsequently entered service with the RAF as EE205, and after spending a useful war, much of it with No.1426 (Enemy Aircraft) Fight conducting fighter affiliation trials, it was unfortunately destroyed in a gale at RAF Sealand, in Cheshire, where it was in storage after being selected for permanent preservation. Broadfield Down had actually been planned as Colerne's second satellite aerodrome, but when it was finally opened in January 1942 the need for it had passed and so, under the new name of Lulsgate Bottom, the facility was taken over by RAF Training Command.

Rationing Extended

By mid-1941 clothing was also in short supply due to the lack of raw materials and the fact that many of the factories had by then converted to manufacturing items necessary for the war effort. Therefore a system of rationing similar to that for food was introduced on 1 June, when each person was given 66 coupons to last for a 12-month period. Although hats and men's braces were not rationed, sheets had to be added to the list as women were finding them a useful source of material from which to make their own clothes. Newspapers and Government pamphlets gave tips on how

to make clothing last longer by careful washing and mending and the WVS organised Clothing Exchanges where clothes that had been outgrown could be exchanged for larger items. Because of the problems caused by an ageing workforce and the supply of cloth, the industry was unable to meet the clothing ration at its original level, so in the spring of 1942 it was cut to 48 coupons per year, and 'Utility' clothes and footwear introduced. These garments, manufactured in a set number of designs from standardised materials and using a minimum of fabric, were sold at rigorously controlled prices and, not surprisingly, were warmly welcomed by the general public, eventually accounting for some 80 per cent of production.

As well as clothes, footwear was also in short supply owing not only to a lack of rubber, but also to the fact that many factories had switched over to the production of army boots. Neither were many stockings available for the women, forcing fashion-conscious young women to colour their legs with such substances as gravy browning, or to draw a line up the back of the legs to imitate a stocking's seam! In addition to clothing, all manner of kettles, pans and buckets, domestic electrical appliances, carpets, sports gear, lighters, pens, umbrellas, pencils, musical instruments, pottery and furniture were manufactured as 'Utility' items from mid-1942, and although the production of many non-essential items was banned the Government did permit toys to be sold at Christmas in 1942 and 1943.

The situation regarding food was also deteriorating, and in addition to the items already on 'points', dried fruit, rice, sago, tapioca, pulses, canned fruit, meat, fish, vegetables, tomatoes and peas, condensed milk and breakfast cereal, syrup and treacle, biscuits, oatflakes and rolled oats, were all put on ration by the time the Japanese entered the war in December 1941. This, however, was not the end of the matter as the final act in the food-rationing saga in fact took place in July 1942, when a 'personal points' scheme for chocolate and sweets was introduced, a great blow to a whole generation of youngsters! With so many items of food, clothing, soap, household items and even tooth brushes in limited supply, or even impossible to obtain, the phrase 'under the counter' took on a special wartime meaning, especially as this form of favourtism to a shopkeeper's wealthier clientele was difficult to separate from the 'black market' proper. It was not particularly difficult for the local butcher or grocer to claim rations for any of his customers who happened to be away on holiday, or even newly deceased, while such things as cheese, which seems to have particularly repelled a number of customers, could often be reserved, not for strangers who might well be Ministry of Food spies, but rather for the most-valued customers. Another unofficial source of scarce or rationed food was through unscrupulous farmers and small-holders, while the system of supplying restaurants was also open to abuse.

In addition, a good deal of more or less innocent bargaining also went on, but due to the secret nature of so many of these unofficial transactions details of them are not to be found in official statistics, and relatively few seem to have reached the courts. Lord Woolton, the Minister of Food from April 1940 until November 1943, believed that the efforts of the undercover inspectors from the Ministry's Licensing and Enforcement Divisions, combined with orders which enabled courts of law to impose fines of up to £500, with or without two years' imprisonment, plus three times the total capital involved in any 'black market' transaction, effectively deterred such activity and ensured that the amount of food finding its way onto the 'black market' was insignificant in relation to total supplies.

For the first two and a half years of the war private motorists in Britain had been allowed a small ration of fuel of a type called 'Pool', introduced in September 1939 when all existing brands of petrol were merged into a single type. This situation, however, changed dramatically in March 1942 when even this concession was withdrawn, after which date only essential users, such as doctors, were allowed fuel. This resulted in many private cars being laid up on blocks for the duration, although it should be remembered that at that time only about one in 10 persons owned a car! Nevertheless, Bristol's buses and trams were kept running as normally as possible, but with other forms of road transport limited by the petrol shortages some commercial concerns converted vehicles to run on coal gas often contained in a large bag mounted on the roof, but this was never really a successful alternative. As industrial vehicles were essential for the war effort, many lorries were requisitioned by the Government, and although for reasons of safety and economy speed limits were reduced to 20mph in built-up areas, the emergency services were exempted from this regulation. With road transport disrupted many people depended on bicycles for transport, and although trains still ran, some preferred to travel on these only at night, as the railways were considered a prime target for enemy bombers.

The Home Guard Goes Mobile

By the summer of 1941 the overall military situation had altered to such an extent that the idea of what the Home Guard might realistically achieve in the event of an invasion had to be completely reviewed, something explained by John Brophy in his article which was published by the *Sunday Graphic* in May 1941. 'Rightly or wrongly, many feel that the Home Guard is not being asked or trained to do all it might do. They feel that an undue emphasis is being placed on the duty to observe and report: the emphasis was right in 1940 but wrong today. What they have in mind is that the Home Guard is now ready to tackle, in this or any other order, airborne troops, tanks and dive bombers. That is how they see the job confronting us. To do that job effectively all we need is the right weapons, which cannot be delivered too fast, and more emphasis placed on our local striking power than on limitations we have outgrown.'

As this sentiment was widely felt, changes soon followed, and during July 1941 new plans were drawn up in Bristol which involved setting

A close-up view of the pill box alongside the railway line above Gipsy Patch Lane, Patchway. Normally this would have been manned by Home Guard personnel from the adjoining BAC works. *(Author's Collection)*

up a Defence Committee to assume control of the city's affairs if the enemy actually reached its gates. Consequently, Bristol was divided into five Defence Areas, West, North, East, South, and the Inner Keep, a central portion over which the Defence Committee was to preside to the bitter end. In each of the remaining four a sub-defence committee was established, while the Bristol Fort and Zone commander was confirmed as Colonel A.F. Chapman, with Lieutenant Colonel N.G. Gibson as his deputy, their headquarters being established at 32 Park Row, Clifton. As part of the development of the defensive scheme many battalions and companies had 'battle headquarters' selected and equipped for use in time of emergency, all of which were in telephone communication with each other, the two forward Observation Posts, and the normal Battalion Headquarters. The role of the Home Guard which had, to date, been entirely static was now made more mobile and defence in depth using a system of defended localities was adopted, with a quarter of the troops manning these being trained to move at very short notice.

Towards the end of 1941 and during 1942 three more Gloucestershire Home Guard Battalions were raised locally, the 15th (Bristol GPO), 16th (Bristol) and 18th (Filton), these being formed from personnel of the Post Office in the region, the largest industrial and commercial undertakings in central Bristol, and the Bristol Aeroplane Company at Filton. To create these units the existing platoons in which they were serving, parts of existing formations, were transferred into the new works battalions. Although the number of volunteers who had come forward to serve in these

A close up view of the pill box beside the railway bridge at Gipsy Patch Lane, Patchway, another put in place for the protection of the BAC works. *(Author's Collection)*

battalions were sufficient, and a certain degree of encouragement to join the Home Guard had been given by their managements, it was not easy to persuade the recruits that the proper way to defend their premises was not by sitting and sticking a rifle through a window, but by the use of defended localities several hundred yards away!

On 16 February 1942 the Home Guard became part of the Armed Forces of the Crown on an unpaid basis and subject to Military Law and the Army Act when mustered to resist invasion. It also became a partly conscript force, into which male civilians aged from 18 to 51 could be directed, being thereafter required to attend for up to 48 hours training or other duty a month under penalty of a month in prison or a £10 fine. The right of a volunteer to resign was also withdrawn and from February they, like the directed men, were obliged to stay in until victory or until they reached 65 years of age. The directed recruits as a whole, except in the case of the young men under the age of 21, proved a great contrast to the original volunteers and in a large number of cases men unsuited by their civilian employment were sent to the battalions. In consequence, there were continual difficulties in securing their attendance for training, and the lack of available man power in the later stages of the war brought about continual re-combing of men previously exempted, some of whom failed entirely to accept their responsibilities to their country. However, the situation was somewhat eased by the admission of woman volunteers to their ranks in April 1942, and the Woman's Home Guard Auxiliary reached a remarkably high standard of efficiency in a very short time, thereafter giving invaluable service as drivers, telephonists, clerks and in the Headquarters Intelligence Sections.

Entertaining the Locals

With no sign of an early end to the war, the need for manpower intensified leaving much of the responsibility for keeping the country's vital services running to women, and men nearing retirement age. Consequently, from 1941 men aged over 41, as well as young unmarried women, were required to register at their local Labour Exchanges, from where they were directed into war work, and later this procedure was applied to all women between 19 and 48 years of age who had no children to look after. Finally, in 1943, women between 48 and 50 were obliged to register for war work, something that was soon being nicknamed the 'grannies call-up', and although those over the age of 50 were not obliged to assist with the war effort, many joined voluntary organisations such as the WVS and the Red Cross.

As hostilities dragged on it also became obvious that if people were to continue putting the maximum effort into essential war work they must have relaxation of some kind, and listening to the wireless soon became a national institution, with many factories playing *Music While You Work*

Every woman not doing vital work is needed NOW

FULL INFORMATION AT THE NEAREST RECRUITING CENTRE OR YOUR EMPLOYMENT EXCHANGE

and *Workers Playtime* over their loudspeaker systems. At home, the most popular programmes were the 9pm news, and *ITMA* (*It's That Man Again*), featuring comedian Tommy Handley and his team, which was soon attracting 16 million listeners each Thursday evening, while the war correspondents, including Richard Dimbleby, Frank Gillard and Wynford-Vaughan Thomas drew a similar number to *War Report* which was heard every night at the end of the main evening news.

Of the places of public entertainment, the re-opened cinemas probably remained the most popular with long queues often to be seen waiting outside, and although during an air-raid a warning would be flashed onto the screen inviting the audience to take shelter, as the bombing escalated there were so many warnings that many people just ignored them and carried on enjoying the film. The theatres were also very popular and many of these also carried on regardless through the long war years, while during the BBC's stay in Bristol the public were able to attend the live broadcasts of programmes such as *Band Waggon* from the Colston Hall. During 1941 many Bristolians also took advantage the opportunity of listening to visiting military bands, and these included the particularly popular 30th Battalion of the King's Own Yorkshire Light Infantry, as well as the Calgary Highlanders, who arrived in Bristol in August 1941 and attracted great crowds when their pipers played on the Downs and in Eastville Park. Likewise, the band of the RASC gave two excellent concerts in the early summer, while that from the Wiltshire Regiment visited the city in the autumn.

In order to provide the city's civilian workforce and the locally based military personnel with an even better selection of morale-boosting amusements, early 1942 the Bristol City Council entrusted the organisation of public entertainment to an *ad hoc* committee which arranged for an amateur dramatics society to perform on the Downs on weekday evenings and Saturday afternoons in the summer. Besides plays, there were also exhibitions of various kinds, concerts, circuses, lectures in the City Museum and elsewhere, and exhibitions in the Art Gallery and Central Library. Likewise, carnivals were arranged in many of the city's parks and concert parties and entertainers of all types toured local parish halls, while the lunchtime dancing on College Green proved particularly popular. Some idea of the work that went into providing relaxation for Bristolians can be seen by the fact that during the summers of 1942 to 1945 some 2,211,593 people attended 2,944 events held in 30 of the city's parks. Of these, the dance music melody vans entertained some 694,000 people, while the 358 band concerts attracted a further 70,000 or so.

Nationalising the Fire Service

Since the start of the bombing campaign against Britain the Ministry of Home Security had been analysing the effect that the 'Night Blitz' had had on towns and cities throughout the country, and many serious problem were identified. In spite of the fact that the ARP Act of 1937 had required neighbouring fire brigades to work out reinforcing schemes to allow mutual assistance to be given to which ever area was threatened, it was quickly discovered that during major attacks the arrival of more distant crews in fact created serious problems in command, control and communications due to the non-standardisation of equipment, drills, terminology, rank structures and uniforms. Nationalisation was the obvious way to resolve the problem, and this was implemented on 18 August 1941, with the result that Bristol then became part of No.17 Fire Force, the headquarters of which was established at Westbury on Trym. With the establishment of the National Fire Service it was decided that all the existing Supplementary Fire Parties should form part of the general Wardens' Service and should from then on be known as Fire Guards. Formed into teams of three persons, their principal task would be to watch for incendiary bombs and to deal with as many as possible as soon as they fell, so that the fires were unable to get a hold.

The Rockets Arrive

During September 1941 the strengthening of the local air defences also continued and construction of the first two rocket-firing 'Z' sites in the Bristol area was completed that month, all of which were to be initially manned by the 9th Anti-Aircraft 'Z' Regiment. The installation at Easton in Gordano was positioned to cover Avonmouth Docks and that at Bishopsworth for the protection of Bristol Docks, but although a further four sites were also planned only those at Brislington and Abbots Leigh, were ever completed. All the local installations were armed with 3in rockets, these being

One of two gun pits constructed from reinforced concrete blocks built in late 1942 on the Purdown gun site. These were to be used by the 71st. (Gloucestershire) Heavy Anti-Aircraft Home Guard Battery. *(Author's Collection)*

launched in salvoes of 128 to a maximum height of 19,000ft by using 64 twin-projectors per site. Although these 'Z' batteries were well suited to firing barrages, the locations and discharge directions had to be carefully chosen to minimise the danger from falling tailpipes, which could cause as much havoc on the ground as a small German bomb!

As the threat of aerial bombardment was by now much diminished, by the end of 1941 the decision was made to draft some 50,000 men away from Anti-Aircraft Command and to replace them with Home Guard and women ATS personnel. Locally, the Home Guard men were transferred on a geographical basis in relation to the gun positions, those selected becoming part of a new formation, the 71st (Gloucestershire) HAA Battery, Home Guard, while from April 1942 transfers were also made to the 101st to 104th Rocket Batteries to serve on the city's 'Z' sites. To build this organisation up speedily Bristol battalions were called upon to give up large numbers of men, the 16th Battalion, for instance, provided some 800, while the 12th were forced to find 1,250.

The effect of this was to strip a number of the battalions of practically all the fitter and more regularly trained members, except for a limited number of instructors and specialists. This was a very serious blow and, for a time, completely disorganised some of the formations, destroying much of the team spirit that had been so carefully built up over the previous three years. As it was not permissible to transfer complete platoons, the result was that all such formations were disorganised, with some being left with as few as 10 men. To compound the problems, those remaining were either medically less fit or engaged on round-the-clock shift work which largely precluded regular or Sunday training, while there was also a regular heavy wastage of personnel by reason of men being called up for the regular Army, RAF and Navy.

Unfortunately, throughout the war Anti-Aircraft Command also tended to be treated as a reserve for the Army in general, with men constantly being transferred to other formations and theatres of operation, a good example of this being the local 76th Heavy Anti-Aircraft Regiment which started its move from the Bristol area to North Africa in November 1941. In an attempt to maintain manning levels it was therefore decided to recruit women from the Auxiliary Territorial Service to form 'mixed' batteries made up of both men as well as women, the latter carrying out nearly all the duties done by the men except actually firing the guns. As a first step towards this on 22 September the 133rd (M) Heavy Anti-Aircraft Regiment was formed at Clifton, and shortly after women were assigned for service on some 12 heavy anti-aircraft sites around Bristol.

The use of women was also extended to the 'Z' batteries, while female crews from the Women's Auxiliary Air Force took over the responsibility for a number of barrage balloon sites around the city, but not before the somewhat crude living conditions often associated with these had been improved. Nevertheless, the WAAFs still had to endure the weather as well as the danger of attack from the air, and although theirs was one of the hardest jobs undertaken by women during the war, they carried out the complicated balloon operations with all the ease and efficiency of men. In spite of the fact that ATS manning had done much to keep the anti-aircraft units up to strength, even this source eventually started to dry up, so there was great relief in late February 1942 when the first Home Guard volunteers commenced manning Bristol's heavy anti-aircraft guns and at the end of June when they started to take over responsibility for the local 'Z' sites.

The Luftwaffe at Bay

With so few aircraft now available to the Luftwaffe for operations against Britain, very little activity was experienced over the Bristol area during the latter part of 1941, although minelaying around the coasts of Southern England did re-start in September following the transfer of III./KG 30 aling with its Junkers Ju 88s from the Balkans to Northern France. The unit extended its operations to the Bristol Channel and Severn Estuary area in early October, before removing to Norway in December 1941. Locally, as a result of the Gruppe's activities six ships were sunk in the Severn Estuary, and a further one damaged, while on the night of 25 November a man was killed at Oldbury Naite, just north of Bristol, the victim of a stray mine which came down on land.

a sound of victory in the air

Bristol

HERCULES Engines

However, in spite of the fact that so few enemy aircaft were operating over Britain the Germans certainly had not given up the idea of transferring bombers back to Luftflotte 3 when the situation on the Eastern Front allowed, and over in Germany in late December 1941 the Luftwaffe's two original pathfinder units, KGr 100 and III./KG 26 combined together to form KG 100. In mid-February 1942 Ergr.u.Lehr Kdo 100, a small experimental Staffel operating Heinkel 111s, was detached from KGr 100 and sent to France to carry out development work with X and Y-Verfahren under operational conditions. Their first foray over Britain was probably undertaken during the evening of 3 April when suitable cloud cover allowed an experimental daylight precision attack using X-Verfahren to be mounted against the Bristol Aeroplane Company at Filton. Just as the sun was setting the single aircraft approached from the direction of Salisbury, but it was immediately engaged with 38 rounds fired by the local heavy anti-aircraft guns forcing the crew to make a wide turn over Bristol. Four high-explosives were then dropped on the Stockwood 'Starfish' decoy, and a few others in the vicinity of Bitton and Keynsham, before the Heinkel raced back to the safety of France, a somewhat ignominious end to German's last attempt at interrupting production at the local aircraft plants.

Baedeker Bombers over Bristol

A most difficult situation then arose, as following a devastating RAF raid on Lübeck on the night of 28 March, German public opinion began demanding heavy reprisal attacks against British cities. Although few aircraft could be spared from the Russian Front, a small formation of about 80 aircraft was assembled for which Ergr.u.Lehr Kdo 100 using Y-Verfahren were to act as pathfinders. These purely terror attacks were planned to start during the moonlight period at the end of April and were to be concentrated and of short duration in order to minimise British defensive action. The series of RAF raids on Rostock, which began on 23 April, really brought things to a head and as a result the Germans threatened eradication of all British cities listed in Baedeker's tourist guidebook. The campaign, thereafter became known in both Germany and Britain as the 'Baedeker Raids', and the attack sequence opened with operations against Exeter followed on the nights of 25 and 26 April by heavy raids on Bath, a soft target which was completely devoid of anti-aircraft guns or barrage balloons.

For these attacks all bomber units of Luftflotte 3 were called upon to participate, consequently Ergr.u.Lehr Kdo 100 led in not only II. and III./KG 2, and II./KG 40 equipped with the newly introduced Dornier Do 217s, as well as Kü. Fl. Gr. 106 and Kü. Fl. Gr. 506, anti-shipping units flying Junkers Ju 88s, but also for the first time a numbers of crews form the reserve training units IV./KG 2, IV./KG 3, IV./KG 4, IV./KG 30, IV./KG 55 and IV./KG 77, flying an assortment of obsolete Dornier 17s, Heinkel 111s and Junkers 88s. During the first night, 25 April, the Luftwaffe flew a total of 151 bomber sorties to Bath, during which the crews claimed to have dropped 206 tonnes of high explosives and 3,564 incendiaries on the city in the biggest effort against Britain since July 1941. The raid began a little after 11pm, but in spite of the bright moonlight in the target area some of the early arrivals mis-identified their objective completely and bombs were unintentionally dropped on the Brislington area of Bristol, where 18 people were killed and 41 injured. As a result, Bristol's 'Z' sites were able to go into action for the first time, firing a total of 38 rockets, and although the Avonmouth smoke screen was also ignited, an enemy aircraft dive-bombed and machine gunned a Haslar generator and its towing vehicle, putting both out of action.

The following night a further 83 bombers were dispatched to Bath in a repeat operation, but on this occasion the enemy's navigation was better and Bristol was unaffected. By this time, due to the strength of the local air defences, little daylight reconnaissance was possible over the Bristol area, nevertheless on 29 April a modified Messerschmitt Bf 109 single-engined fighter from the reconnaissance unit 3.(F)/123 did succeed in obtaining post-raid cover of Bath, as well as photographing Avonmouth and the Nailsea area, its long-range drop tank being jettisoned at Pill at around midday as the aircraft began its dangerous return flight.

After the raids on Exeter and Bath, came attacks on York, Norwich, and Cowes, all of these being led

MESSERSCHMITT Me 109F
SINGLE-SEAT FIGHTER
Span 32'-7"   Length 29'-9"

Silhouette of the Messerschmitt Bf 109. *(Author's Collection)*

by Epgr.u.Lehr Kdo 100 which, in mid-May, was re-designated Ergr.u.Lehr Kdo 17. In spite of undertaking this work, the unit still found time to carry out a few experimental daylight attacks, and one of these was the attempt against Avonmouth Docks undertaken by seven Heinkels in poor weather on the afternoon of 23 May, using both X and Y-Verfahren. This operation, however, did not go according to plan for on the outward flight 6N+FR flown by the Staffelkäpitan, Hauptmann Siegfried Langer, was forced to crash into the ground near Shaftesbury by a Beaufighter from No.604 Squadron crewed by Wing Commander John Cunningham and Flight Lieutenant C.F. 'Jimmy' Rawnsley, this being accomplished without a shot being fired! From then on matters got worse and only two of the raiders succeeded in penetrating as far as Bristol, where the local heavy guns engaged them with 26 rounds forcing them away from their objective, the nearest bombs falling at Severn Tunnel Junction, some six miles north of Avonmouth.

About this time the wooden Mosquito, a new type of night fighter equipped with the latest Airborne Interception radar and armed with cannons and machine guns, began entering service with Fighter Command. This twin-engined aircraft with a performance considerably better than that of the Beaufighter, was delivered to No.264 Squadron at Colerne during May 1942 and quickly became operational in the defence of Bristol.

During May and June the Luftwaffe busied itself with nocturnal raids on towns and cities in various parts of England, but the end of June 1942 saw a return to more local objectives with Weston-super-Mare being visited on the nights of 27 and 28 June, while during July German activities were directed mainly against ports and the British armaments industry. This new phase started with an attempt on the harbour installations at Bristol early on the morning of 2 July, in which some 46 Dornier 217s from I., II. and III./KG 2, and II./KG 40, are known to have taken part.

Unfortunately for the those participating there was thick haze and 40 per cent cloud cover in the target area, and in spite of the returning aircrews claiming to have attacked Bristol with 20 tonnes of high explosives, the nearest any bombs came to the city were those reported falling at Brean Down just after 2am. Nevertheless, widespread bombing of alternative targets had taken place, particularly along the south and south west coasts, as well as in South Wales, and although an aircraft from II./KG 2 subsequently landed back in France with one crewman killed and one injured following a brush with a night fighter, that was the nearest the defences came to success that night.

A Final Taste of Horror

In spite of all the Germans best efforts, by the end of July the 'Baedeker Raids' had petered out, as the losses caused to the attack force by the ever strengthening British defences were becoming unsustainable. There was, however, still pressure to continue retaliation as the RAF attacks on Germany had become progressively heavier, culminating in the 'Thousand Bomber' raids on Cologne, Essen and Bremen.

One of the few possibilities open to the Germans at this time was to employ their new and experimental Junkers Ju 86R ultra high-altitude bombers. As a brief trial at a research establishment in Germany carried out by the Höhenkampfkommando der Versuchsstelle für Höhenflüge had proved the feasibility of bombing operations from altitudes of around 40,000ft in mid-August the

Silhouette of the Dornier Do 217. *(Author's Collection)*

DORNIER   Do 217
Bomber
Span 62' 5''   Length 56' 6''

The Junkers Ju 86R T5+PM from the Einsatzkommando Ju 86 which attacked Bristol during the morning of 28 August 1942. (via G. Morley)

combat trials unit, Einsatzkommando Ju 86, together with two aircraft, moved to Beauvais in France to commence operations against Britain. The Ju 86R was not particularly fast, nor did it carry any armament, but for its survival relied upon the fact that it could attack from altitudes then considered out of the reach of any British fighter then in service. As there appeared to be little to fear from the defences the attacks were carried out during daytime, although the Ju 86R's offensive load was limited to just a single 250kg bomb.

Operations started with an attack on Camberley on the morning of 24 August, followed by sorties to Southampton and Stanstead, while on 28 August Bristol was targeted. The lone aircraft, bearing the fuselage codes T5+PM, which was commanded by Leutnant Erich Sommer and piloted by Unteroffizier Horst Götz, appeared unannounced over the city at about 9.20am, and a few minutes later its bomb impacted on a Ford 10 car parked in Bristol's Broad Weir. As a result of the subsequent explosion one of three nearby buses was seriously damaged by blast, while petrol from the car's fuel tank was sprayed in a more or less atomized state over the other two which immediately burst into flames. The death toll was horrific, with 45 people being killed, many burnt to death in the blazing buses, with a further 45 injured, and in terms of loss of life this was the single most serious incident to occur in Bristol during World War Two.

This horror was very widely reported, and the following day under the headline 'Day Bombs Fire Three Buses – Children Among the Victims', the *Daily Telegraph* told its readers:

'One bomb dropped by one of two raiders which came in "out of the blue" over Bristol in daylight today caused fairly heavy casualties. It fell near three buses laden with passengers, business people and schoolchildren. The bomb pitched in the road only a few yards from the buses, and bomb fragments riddled them. Almost immediately the buses, their fuel tanks releasing the petrol, burst into flames and the passengers inside were trapped. A building partly collapsed on a street corner was brought down completely. The buses burst into flames so quickly that little could be done for the people inside, though the fire brigades

This was the view up Broad Weir, looking towards Philadelphia Street, on the morning of 28 August 1942. All three buses shattered by the single 250kg bomb can be clearly be seen. *(BUP)*

arrived within little more than a minute. Even as the firemen were playing on the burning wreckage of the building which had collapsed, others were tearing away beams and broken woodwork in the hope of rescuing the occupants.'

In an attempt to counter this new threat several suitably modified Spitfires were issued to the specially formed Special Service Flight at Northolt, near London, and a new control system introduced involving a number of GCI stations in Southern England simultaneously feeding plots of both the intercepting fighter and the high altitude raider to a special area control room. This procedure, code named 'Windgap', was unsuccessfully tried on 11 September, but the following day during an attempt against Cardiff by Götz and Sommer the lone Junkers, from 14./KG 6, as Einsatzkommando Ju 86 had just been redesignated, was intercepted en-route by a specially modified Spitfire flown by Pilot Officer Prince Emanuel Galitzine. For the first time a Ju 86R was engaged in combat, and the crew, who hastily jettisoned their bomb near Salisbury, were lucky to return to France with only one cannon hole through the port wing. So ended the highest air battle ever fought over Britain and one which immediately brought to an end the high altitude bombing experiment.

The Yanks are Here

Following the entry of the United States into the war, American troops had begun arriving in the UK in January 1942, quickly taking over buildings and land provided by the British Government on a lend lease basis. They had not been in the country long when the decision was taken that the majority of them were to be billeted in the Southern Command area, which included Bristol, and when the first American troops sailed into Avonmouth in August 1942 they received a rapturous welcome. Although the US military went on to take over a number of local buildings, of which Clifton College was to become the most important, they also occupied the Lyndon Hotel, and later the

American GIs at Clifton College attempting to fathom the rules of cricket. *(BUP)*

A surviving wartime ward at Frenchay Hospital. *(Author's Collection)*

West of England College of Art which were used as the American Red Cross Club, for white troops. Americans were also to be found at Frenchay and Ashton Court, while another camp was established at Bedminster to guard mountain of stores held in the former bonded tobacco warehouse which had become part of G-38, the biggest American supply depot in the country occupying some fourteen sites in and around the city. In addition, accommodation was also provided in Shirehampton Park for those working at Avonmouth Docks, at Filton for the men assembling aircraft there, and at Patchway for a communications unit, while some Americans were housed at Muller's Orphanage on Ashley Down, at Brislington, and at camp established near the Greyhound Track at Knowle. Other parts of Bristol were also touched by the American presence including Durdham Down, which served as a vehicle park, and Ashton Court Park where tanks, trucks and other vehicles were stored.

Some of the first Americans to arrive in the West Country served with the army medical units that had started to occupy Bristol Corporation's redundant emergency hospital at Frenchay, but neither the 152nd Station Hospital, the 77th Evacuation Hospital, or the 2nd Evacuation Hospital, stayed there for very long. The same, however, could not be said of the 298th General Hospital, a formation affiliated to the University of Michigan, which took over the base on 13 November 1942 and remained at Frenchay until 16 May 1944, before handing over to 100th General Hospital. Not surprisingly, the Americans found the existing facilities too small for their needs and quickly expanded the site by erecting numerous Nissan-type huts to house a motor pool, stores and the hospital's personnel, so that by late 1943 it had developed into a large complex boasting 27 brick-built wards.

CHAPTER 9

ONWARDS TO VICTORY

January 1943 to May 1945

As the Luftwaffe's reprisal attacks of 1942, directed mainly against unprotected cities, had revealed the urgent need of coordinating the efforts and resources of the Fire Guard and the NFS, the idea was born that this huge organisation could provide a formidable fire defence in conjunction with the NFS. This lead, in February 1943, to the adoption of the Fire Guard Plan under which the sole responsibility for reporting fires due to enemy action was transferred from the Wardens to the Fire Guard Service which, it was hoped, would provide a reliable and constant communication system invulnerable to air attack. Bristol threw itself whole-heartedly into the scheme, and by the middle of the summer 403 instructors were ready to train the Fire Guards in the use of NSF equipment.

During the winter and spring of 1942–43 the local defence committees were also consolidated and strengthened, and in order to test the mechanism and to make sure that both the defence committee and its divisional sub-committees knew their business, a series of exercises was arranged. At first these were confined to particular divisions of Bristol, but were later held for the whole of the city. It was the general practice on these occasions to entrust the attack to the field army and the defence to the garrison and Home Guard, with all the Civil Defence services fully extended. The first large exercise took place on 1 and 2 November and was intended to test the system to the south of the River Avon by an attack on Whitchurch aerodrome and South Bristol, while on 7 and 8 March 1943 a second exercise, code named 'Eastern' was held to check the efficiency of the Bristol East Division, and here the battle took place almost completely in built-up areas.

'Exercise Thunder', the largest of the series, took place between 15 and 17 May 1943, and was the first of its kind to be held in the country. Because of this it was intended that in so far as possible Bristol should be confronted with invasion conditions and as the entire population of the city was expected to participate, all residents had to receive the necessary instruction. In the exercise against Charmy Down

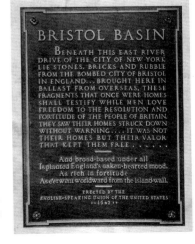

This plaque was erected in New York in 1942 to commemorate the fact that many ships returning from Bristol used rubble from the blitzed city as ballast. It now stands on a building named 'Waterside Plaza'. An identical plaque was set up in Bristol but as over the years this became lost, in 1986 a replacement was provided by BBC Radio Bristol. *(BUP)*

airfield, designed to test the defences of the aerodrome, the Bristol battalions were used as the attacking force and a spirited battle developed against the defenders, the Bath Home Guard. Local rivalry added a spice to the occasion and fists and arms were used in a most unorthodox fashion, before Brigadier Churchill, who was in command of the operation, brought the battle to a close! These sort of exercises were particularly important as by this time, if the need had arisen, the defence of the city would have been undertaken almost entirely by the Home Guard acting under the operational control of the garrison commander.

During 1943 new weapons also began arriving in large numbers, and by the autumn the Home Guard was at last on its way to becoming a force to be reckoned with, although its members were still expected to make do with a number of unorthodox, problematic, and even potentially dangerous weapons, as well as obsolete standard service issue rifles and machine guns. This is well illustrated by a list of weapons held early in 1944 by the 16th Battalion for the defence of central Bristol.

'Over 11,000 rifles, 50 Browning Light Automatic Rifles, 695 Sten guns, 26 Lewis Guns, 11 Browning machine guns, 4 Vickers machine guns, 20 Boys 0.55" anti-tank rifles, 60 grenade firing rifles with discharger caps; 16 Smith 3" Guns with trailers, 10 Spigot Mortars and 26 Northover Projectors.'

In addition they also had available about 11,000 grenades of various patterns, over 460,000 rounds of small arms ammunition, and approximately 5,000 rounds for larger calibre weapons. As

The bomb crater on the quayside at Welsh Back, now incorporated into the general dockside scene. It was made by a high explosive bomb on the night of 2 January 1941. *(Author's Collection)*

The iron tablet set into the stone work in the old bomb crater on Welsh Back. It reads: 'This quay-side was destroyed by a bomb in 1941'. *(Author's Collection)*

well as the standard No. 36 Mills Bomb, the grenade stock also included No. 76 Self-Igniting Phosphorous (SIP) Grenades, or 'Sticky Bombs' the first weapon universal to the Home Guard and one primarily intended for anti-vehicle use, as well as the No. 68 Rifle Grenade. This latter device was designed to be fired as an anti-tank projectile from the barrel of a modified rifle but, through a mixture of poor training in its use and lack of quality control, the weapon was inaccurate and developed a bad reputation among some units for its premature explosion!

Likewise, of the larger weapons, the Northover Projector which also fired SIP grenades, contained so many design faults as to render it not only useless under combat conditions, but also positively dangerous to those charged with using it. Although the Spigot Mortar was certainly more imposing than the Northover Projector, its anti-tank ammunition proved to have such an insensitive impact fuse that it would pass right through an unarmoured vehicle or hit the ground without exploding, while if it did go off the remains of the tail fins had a nasty habit of hurtling back towards the gun crew! The third type of sub-artillery issued to the Home Guard was the Smith Gun, opinion of which was far from favourable, for it had a very low muzzle velocity, was inaccurate, and had an effective range of not more than 300yd.

By the end of 1943 the Bristol Sub-Area, embraced not only the city itself, known by then as the 'Bristol Fort with Inner Keep' but also four other 'forts' outside the main area, as well as a considerable area of Somerset to the south and west, all of which was garrisoned by the Home Guard which, for the purpose, employed eight Gloucestershire (Bristol) Battalions plus elements of 7th Somerset (Long Ashton) Battalion. Outside the city itself the 10th Gloucestershire Battalion was responsible for 'Whitchurch Fort' which embraced Bristol Airport, the 13th for the 'Filton Fort', which protected the vital aircraft plant, and the 14th for 'Fort Severn Section' which covered the dock complex at Avonmouth, while 'Fort Portishead', established around the harbour and power station, was the responsibility of the 7th Somerset Battalion, a unit which also manned the 'South Bristol Out Post Zone', based at Wraxall House.

Preparing for 'D-Day'

Clifton College, whose scholars had been evacuated to Cornwall in February 1941, played many parts during the war and after being transferred to the Americans in 1942 was used by a number of

St Mary Redcliffe churchyard. The plaque reads: 'On Good Friday, 11th April 1941, this tramline was thrown over the adjoining houses by a high explosive bomb which fell on Redcliff Hill. It is left to remind us of how narrowly the church escaped destruction in the war 1939–45'. *(Author's Collection)*

their units before the main body of the Headquarters Staff, First US Army, arrived there from Governor's Island, New York, on 20 October 1943. Commanded initially by Lt Gen. George Grunert, and from February 1944 by Lt. Gen. Omar N. Bradley, the First Army was to spearhead the invasion of Europe. During its time in Bristol the headquarters staff were primarily engaged in secret planning for 'D-Day' and supervising the training and re-equipment of many units under its jurisdiction. The school soon became the hub of an extensive communications network, and several large houses in Clifton, Stoke Bishop, Westbury on Trym and Henleaze were also requisitioned to provide additional accommodation, with General Bradley himself residing at 'The Holmes', near the Downs. Arrangements were also for liaison aircraft of the Army's HQ Air Section to use the college sports field at Beggars Bush Lane, near Abbots Leigh, as an airstrip.

Avonmouth Docks had first become involved with the Americans when coloured troops were taken there to learn the business of the dockers before being shipped out to North Africa following the landing there by US on 8 November 1942. Although Avonmouth began receiving dismantled and crated aircraft from the United States in November 1943, mainly as deck cargo on oil tankers, in was not until 27 December of that year that the first batch arrived for local re-assembly at the newly established facility, USAAF Station 803 at Filton. Three units of the IX Air Service Command of the 9th Air Force were to be based there, forming the IX Base Aircraft Assembly Depot. The first to arrive was No.21 USAAF Mobile Repair and Reclamation Squadron which moved in on 28 November 1943, followed by No.22 on 29 November, and No.36 on 3 December. USAAF personnel at Filton eventually numbered some 500, but to begin with many of the airmen were put 'under canvas'. Very soon, however, the facilities were increased and included four Butler Combat hangers, which were transportable sheds resembling enlarged 'Robin' types.

The aircraft unloaded at Avonmouth were taken by road to Filton, where, during their six month stay the Americans re-assembled numerous machines of various types, including the P-38, P-47, P-51,

Royal Edward Dock, Avonmouth. *(NFS)*

A-20, AT-6, UC-64 and UC-78, before they were flight tested and delivered to the rapidly increasing number of operational 9th Air Force units in southern England. So efficient was the operation at Avonmouth, that by early 1944 the majority of American aircraft shipped to Britain were coming in through the docks, and by the end of the war the port had handled some 2,167 aircraft of all types. This facility obviously had to be shielded from the prying eyes of the Luftwaffe and so, on 24 February, a new Avonmouth smoke screen consisting of 24 Esso generators was ignited by the men of the 79th Chemical Smoke Generator Company, US Army, in order to provide a daylight demonstration. This was reasonably satisfactory, but it was suggested the generators should be further away from the area they were protecting, so as not to affect the unloading of ships in the docks, while at the same time increasing their numbers and spacing them closer together.

Was that the Baby Blitz?

Towards the end of 1943 Hitler, infuriated by the the terrible pounding that the RAF was inflicting on Germany's cities during the battles of the Ruhr, Hamburg and Berlin, ordered the Luftwaffe to retaliate against Britain and although it had originally been intended to bombard the south of England with V1 flying bombs a series of technical problems conspired to postpone this course of action. Consequently, on 28 November 1943, it was announced that the attacks were to be undertaken by conventional bombers, and to accomplish this, in December 1943 Luftflotte 3 was reinforced mainly with units withdrawn from Italy, so that within a month it possessed a little over 500 bombers. Although this force was made up mainly of Junkers Ju 88s and Dornier Do 217s, some 20 per cent of it comprised Junkers Ju 188s, Heinkel He 177s and Messerschmitt Me 410s, all recently introduced types, and once again the Germans were to rely heavily upon 'expert'

The Junkers Ju 188A medium bomber. *(via G. Morley)*

pathfinders crews to guide the majority of these aircraft to their objectives. However, this was perhaps a little over optimistic as I./KG 66, the unit chosen for this task, had in fact been formed around 15./KG 6, as Ergr.u.Lehr Kdo 17 had been re-titled a little over a year before, and during their last foray over the West Country back in the summer of 1942 they had proved incapable of locating Avonmouth Docks in daylight, even with their electronic aids to assist them! Nevertheless, while carrying out their new duties this Y-Verfahren equipped formation was also to work in conjunction with the 'Illuminators' of II./KG 2, and together they were to mark the route and the targets by using an elaborate system of sky and ground markers.

The offensive, which had been planned to open during the full moon period in December 1943 was, in fact, delayed until mid-January 1944, when operations began with an attack on London, the

The Heinkel He 177A, the Germans' unsuccessful attempt at producing a heavy bomber. *(via G. Morley)*

capital continuing to be the target throughout February and into March. These missions, however, produced most unsatisfactory results due to a combination of inaccurate navigation and target marking, unreliable aircraft, strong defences, poorly trained aircrews, and the almost immediate transfer back to Italy of nearly 100 aircraft urgently needed to counter the Allied landings. As a consequence 'Unternehmen Steinbock', or the 'Baby Blitz' as it soon became known in Britain, was already doomed to failure and although in mid-March the Luftwaffe began switching their efforts to harbours on the east and south coasts from which any invasion of mainland Europe would have to be launched, the campaign had by this time degenerated into a complete disaster.

This concentration on the ports ensured that during the next two months Bristol, through which so much American equipment was now flowing, was targeted three times by large formations of bombers. There was, however, little cause for concern, for so ineptly were these attacks carried out that Bristolians found themselves in the bizarre situation of only knowing that their city had been the Luftwaffe's main objective when they either read the official German communiqués in the newspaper, or heard them on the radio.

In an attempt to counter the 'Baby Blitz', on 26 March 1944 No.219 Squadron, equipped with the de Havilland Mosquito, was moved to Colerne, just in time to take an active part in defending Bristol from the first raid mounted against it since late 1942. This operation took place the following night, carried out it appears by the Ju 188s of I./KG 66 and II./KG 2 leading in the Do 217s from I. and III./KG 2, the Ju 88s of I.,II., and III./KG 6, II. and III./KG 30, and I. and II./KG 54, and possibly a few unreliable He 177s from I/.KG 100. In an attempt to hinder the defences in the Bristol area a co-ordinated attack was also mounted against nearby night-fighter airfields by the Me 410 fighter-bombers of I./KG 51. A far as the Luftwaffe was concerned, at least on this occasion the objective seemed to have been reached, as upon their return 116 of the 139 crews dispatched claimed to have attacked Bristol between 11.58pm and 0.13am with 100 tonnes of bombs, among which were a number of the recently introduced large phosphorus incendiaries and some anti-personnel bombs. The following day Radio Hamburg told listeners in Britain that:

'Last night's German air attack was directed against the West Coast port of Bristol. A great number of H.E. and thousands of incendiaries were dropped on Bristol in a sharp attack which lasted half an hour. The incendiaries were dropped in a novel way and returning crews said big fires were caused.'

Later the German News Agency reported that:

'The concentrated attack by strong formations of bombers' had caused extensive damage and that 'the British A.A. defences in the South of England suffered what is probably their greatest defeat last night. They were taken completely by surprise and, although the A.A. barrage was very sharp on the coast and over Bristol itself, it was nothing like the barrage in recent raids on London. There were sharp encounters with night fighters and at least two were shot down. Crews of the large number of heavy and fast bombers were able to find their targets at Bristol by means of special devices.'

This, in fact, was all complete fantasy, and in reality the few aircraft that managed to get anywhere near the city were all led astray by inaccurate target marking. As a result incidents were

Bristol power station on the Floating Harbour, providing power for the tram network, target GB 50 51. Document c, the plan, prepared September 1939. This target is better known as the Counterslip generating station.

reported over the whole of Southern England, from Hastings to North Somerset, the closest bombs to Bristol actually falling around Winford, in Somerset, some four miles south of the nearest harbour installations. In spite of all the grandiose claims subsequently issued by the German Ministry of Propaganda it should really have been a night for them to forget as 13 valuable bombers had been lost, of which ten failed to return, and three crashed in occupied France. RAF fighters flying in defence of the West Country fared particularly well and accounted for two Ju 88s, B3+FK from I./KG 54 which came down near Yeovil, and 4D+EP from II./KG 30 which fell at Berkeley, as well as an 'illuminator' Do 217, U5+EN from II./KG 2, shot down near Wells.

The ground defences also actively engaged the raiders, the local heavy guns firing a total of 540 rounds and the 'Z' Batteries a further 91 rockets. Of the units involved, 670 Battery, 133rd (Mixed) HAA Regiment at Weston-super-Mare claimed to have brought down the Ju 88 from the Geschwader Stab/KG 54, which crashed near Wedmore at 11.55pm, although the three surviving crewmen from B3+UA put their demise down to a fire that had already developed in a faulty engine!

For nearly a month the skies over the Bristol area remained clear of Luftwaffe aircraft until the local harbour installations were once more chosen as the target, this time for the 117 aircraft dispatched on the night of 23 April, an operation again carried out in parallel with attack on nearby

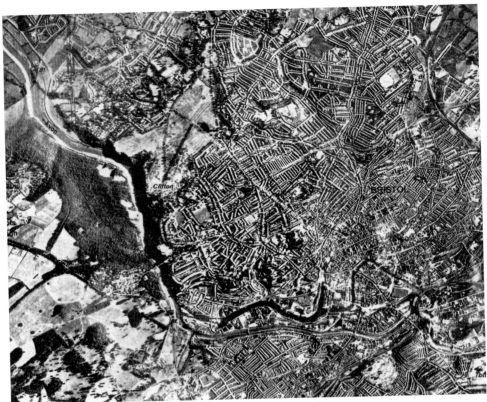

Bristol Waterworks, target GB 53 51. Document b, the photograph, taken at about 7.30am on the morning of 30 June 1940 by an aircraft from Aufklärungsgruppe Ob.d.L. and issued in January 1943. This is in fact the Victoria Reservoir at Clifton.

night-fighter airfields by I./KG 51. The bomber force, which seems to have been drawn from I./KG 2, now operating Ju 188s, as well as III./KG 2, I., II. and III./KG 6, II. and III./KG 30, I. and III./KG 54, and I./KG 100, together with some Ju 88s from the reserve training unit IV./KG 101, were as usual to be led by the pathfinders of I./KG 66 and the 'illuminators' of II./KG 2. Of those taking part, some 93 crews subsequently claimed to have attacked the target with 59.3 tonnes of high explosives and 79.4 tonnes of incendiaries, but just as on 27 March not a single bomb fell in Bristol, the nearest being that reported at Batheaston, some 13 miles east of the city. With the attackers spread out across Southern England German losses were again very heavy, and a total of ten aircraft failed to return, with a further four coming down in France. Many of these were accounted for by RAF fighters, including Ju 88 4D+FM from II./KG 30 which was brought down at Hill Deverill, in Wiltshire, by a Mosquito. Nevertheless, the complete failure of the operation did nothing to stop the German News Agency from subsequently claiming that 'Strong formations of German bomber formations last night made a concentrated attack on Bristol. Fierce fires and destruction were caused to the target areas.'

Unfortunately as by this time Colerne airfield had become heavily involved in the build up for 'D-Day' and its original satellite, Charmy Down, had been USAAF Station 487 since November 1943, it was decided that Zeals, Colerne's old poorly drained and difficult to use forward operating base near Shaftesbury, should once again operate fighter aircraft. The plan was that it should house two night-fighter squadrons for the protection of the West Country, and the first of these, No.488 (New Zealand) equipped with Mosquitoes, arrived on 12 May 1944. This proved to be a wise move for although during late April and early May shipping at Portsmouth and Plymouth had been targeted, on the night of 14 May Luftwaffe bombers again ventured over Britain, their crews briefed to destroy the harbour installations at Bristol. The 91 raiders, which it is thought came from I. and III./KG 2, I. and II./KG 6, II. and III./KG 30, I. and III./KG 54, and I./KG 100, converged on Guernsey from where the pathfinders of I./KG 66 and the 'illuminators' of II./KG 2 led them directly to Bristol, upon which 68 crews subsequently reported dropping 163 tonnes of high

The Canon's Marsh Gas Works on the Floating Harbour, target GB 52 51. Document b, the photograph, taken at about 3.15pm on the afternoon of 26 November 1940 by an aircraft from Aufklärungsgruppe Ob.d.L. and issued in December 1942. Smoke can clearly be seen rising from the smouldering premises alongside the docks two days after the first big raid.

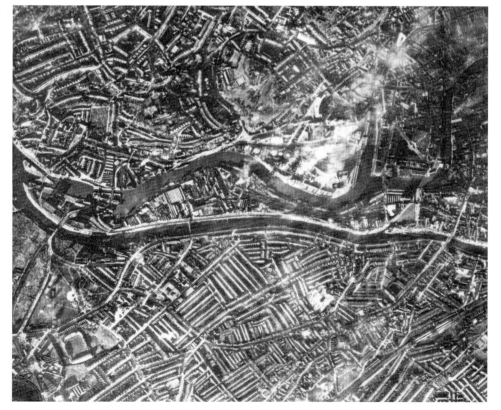

explosives between 1.50 and 2.25am. As was now common practice, a further 15 aircraft from I./KG 51 also made for the local night-fighter airfields at which an additional 4.65 tonnes of bombs were said to have been aimed. These reports again caused the German News Agency to issue a most misleading communiqué, in which they stated that 'Bristol was attacked by strong formations of German heavy bombers. The attack was a very sharp one. At about 2am the German 'planes arrived over their target and dropped a great quantity of explosive and incendiary bombs.'

The true situation was, however, very different for in spite of the German claims only five bombs actually fell that night anywhere within the Bristol city boundary. These, in fact, impacted in the Headley Park area, and over at Kings Weston where at 2am a searchlight site was hit killing Gunner David Winder of 455 Battery, 68th Searchlight Regiment, the last person to lose his life in Bristol as a result of enemy action during World War Two. By contrast, German losses were again completely unsustainable and total of 13 aircraft were destroyed, of which 11 failed to return and two crashed in France, many of the raiders again falling to the guns of the British night-fighters. Over the West during the night Mosquito night interceptors from Zeals are known to have shot down two of these over Somerset, the Ju 188, 3E+LK from I./KG 2, which crashed at Temple Combe, and the Do 217,

The Cattle Market just south of Temple Meads Station, target GB 56 55. Document b, the photograph, taken by a Junkers 88 of 3.(F)/123 at 11.08am on 7 September 1940 and issued in November 1942. While taking this photograph the crew also dropped five high-explosive bombs near the City Docks.

U5+MR from III./KG 2, which came down near Yeovilton, while elsewhere in Southern England other RAF squadrons were equally successful, the excellent results being obtained for the loss of just one RAF pilot. As well as the fighters, other elements of the local air defences had also been in action, with the heavy anti-aircraft guns firing 1,107 rounds and the 'Z' batteries discharging 207 rockets, the last shots fired in anger in the Bristol area during World War Two.

Dismantling the Local Defences

For the inhabitants of the city and surrounding districts the trial by combat was at an end, the 'All Clear' at 3.07am on the morning of 15 May 1944 marking the departure of the last German bomber to threaten the area in a conflict that had lasted since mid-June 1940 and cost the Luftwaffe 96 aircraft lost in operations against Bristol. During the rest of the month the attacks continued against the ports where the forces were concentrating for the invasion of France, and so a number of places along the south coast were targeted during this period. However, this proved to be the final gasp of the 'Baby Blitz' and the raids on the West Country were not continued into June, the surviving aircraft being required to counter the Allied landings on the Continent which finally began on 'D-Day', 6 June 1944.

The retreat of the Luftwaffe away from the battle front soon rendered the Bristol area's air defences redundant, resulting in many of personnel and much of the equipment being transferred to the eastern side of the country, or sent to support the army in France. The first element to be withdrawn was the local bomb disposal unit which moved to Weymouth at the end of June. Shortly after, on 12 July Bristol's barrage balloons were hauled down for the last time, while 1 September saw the closure of all radio countermeasures and decoy sites in the West Country. The next to go was the Home Guard which was stood down on 1 November, followed on 12 December by all anti-aircraft weapons in the Bristol Gun Defended Area being declared non-operational after having fired around 59,000 rounds over a five year period. With the threat of an air attack lifted it also became possible to relax the lighting restrictions, and so it was on 17 September 1944 that the 'black-out' finally came to an end, to be replaced with a 'dim-out' which allowed limited street lighting to be re-introduced and a normal drawn curtain to be used to obscure a lighted window, nevertheless, full illumination was still not permitted until 23 April 1945.

The Drill Hall, Old Market Street. This was the home of the Headquarters Company, 16th. (Bristol) Battalion, Home Guard, and it was also here that the first black American troops to arrive in Bristol were billeted. *(Author's Collection)*

Farewell to our American Allies

As they had a vital role to play in the invasion, immediately before it commenced the First US Army Headquarters had departed from Bristol, although General Bradley had made sure that his 'Stars & Stripes' flag remained behind as a lasting momento, hoping that it might be flown from the flag-pole on every Independence Day. The place of the First US Army at Clifton College was taken by the Headquarters Staff, Ninth US Army under General William H. Simpson, the main body of which arrived at Gourock, near Glasgow, on 28 June, before being brought by train to Bristol, where they remained until 9 August 1944 when they began moving to Normandy by way of Southampton Docks.

When they had first arrived in Bristol many coloured American servicemen were billeted at the Drill Hall, in Old Market, and these included Joe Louis, the boxer, who as a physical training instructor was sent to Bristol to boost the morale of the non-white troops. These men were later housed at Muller's Orphanage, while a club for them was also established in the then vacant building of the Clergy Daughters School in Great George Street. As the American troops were always separated into coloured and white fighting units, housed in separate camps, and given separate entertainment facilities, it is not surprising that at times this situation gave rise to animosity. Bristol was not immune from this, and matters finally came to a head after trouble had been simmering for about a week, the underlying grievance being that the coloured soldiers felt the way the recreation areas of the city had been divided up was unfair, as that they had been allocated the use of the least desirable pubs.

The whole situation finally erupted out of control in Park Street and Great George Street area on Saturday 15 July when, after white servicemen objected to the large number of coloured troops gathered there, brawling broke out. Over 400 coloured and white Americans were involved and it took 120 military police to break it up, the coloured troops being marched off down Park Street to the Centre where trucks were waiting to take them back to camp. Unfortunately, on the way down, panic broke out as military policemen began using their clubs, and in the mêlée that followed a coloured soldier who stabbed an MP with his knife was shot in the legs. In an attempt to contain the fighting, which by then had become very serious, buses were drawn across the side roads, but in the ensuing violence one man was killed and several were seriously injured. The authorities then acted decisively, and in order to defuse the situation and prevent a further confrontation between the ethnic groups, Bristol was placed under military curfew for the next few days.

Meanwhile, as a result of the combat of a different nature by then taking place on the Continent, for the Americans based at Frenchay Hospital a period of intense activity began early the following month, shortly before the 100th General Hospital was sent over to France and replaced by the 117th General Hospital. This involved the facility having to deal with the large number of injured soldiers that were arriving in the continual stream of Dakotas by then operating between Filton airfield and the continental battle front. Some idea of the task that faced them can be seen by the fact that during the period 5 August to 31 December a total of 4,954 patients were discharged from Frenchay, either back to duty, to another hospital for further observation and treatment, to rehabilitation centres, or to America. During this same period, nearly 1,100 patients were decorated at special ceremonies held in the hospital, and among the awards presented were 114 Oak Leaf Clusters, two Silver Stars

The wartime wards still in use at Frenchay Hospital. *(Author's Collection)*

and numerous Purple Hearts. Fortunately, by early 1945 the war in Europe was drawing to an end, and on 6 July, nearly two months after the cessation of hostilities, the 117th were relieved at Frenchay by 52nd General Hospital a unit which, on 17 August, finally handed the site back to the Bristol Health Committee, acting on behalf of the Ministry of Health.

On the whole the American who served in the Bristol area seemed to have left with fond memories of the city, and after the conflict had ended General Bradley sent a letter to Clifton College in which he wrote: 'It may be of interest to you to know that most of the actual command planning for the assault of the American Forces on the beaches of Normandy was carried out in the School House of Clifton College. We held several very important conferences there with the Allied Commanders of the assault forces. Two weeks before "D-Day", commanders of our American assault divisions and brigades met in Clifton for a last-minute review, and briefing of the plan. Many of them left from there to the ports where they loaded their troops into crafts for the invasion. Clifton College will always occupy a very favoured spot in our memories. We like to recall the pleasant days we spent with your people of Bristol in the valued buildings of your institution. You compliment us greatly in associating our activities in this war to those accomplishments of your own Field Marshal Haig in the last. Certainly the associations of American and British troops in this war will contribute heavily to the fine understanding that unites our nations in peace as well as in war.'

General John C.H. Lee, who had masterminded the movement of supplies for the US invasion forces, also seems to have enjoyed his time in Bristol and wrote a similar letter of thanks to the Lord

Lieutenant Colonel Denholm, the officer commanding the 117th General Hospital, receives a small Union Flag as a token of friendship from Lieutenant Colonel C.O. Worth of the 18th. (Gloucestershire) Battalion, Home Guard, which was based at Filton airfield. *(BUP)*

Mayor. However, a mere communication was not enough for the General, and so on 21 June 1946 he returned to Bristol to receive an Honorary Degree from Winston Churchill, Chancellor of the University, while that evening he went to Avonmouth to personally thank the dockers and other members of the workforce for the great contribution the port had made to the Allied victory.

Counting the Cost

With the war over and many Luftwaffe documents in Allied hands it became possible for the first time to make an accurate assessment of just what they had achieved in their operations against Bristol, during which 1,237 tonnes of high explosive and oil bombs, plus 248 tonnes of incendiaries had been aimed at the city during the course of 10 significant attacks. Not surprisingly, with German records showing that between August 1940 and June 1941 Bristol was the fifth most heavily bombed city in the country, with only London, Liverpool, Birmingham and Plymouth receiving more

attention, the most obvious effect of the bombing campaign was on the townscape. In retrospect, Bristol's position in the Luftwaffe's catalogue of destruction is well illustrated by the fact that at the end of the war the City Council announced that over 89,000 properties had been destroyed or damaged by enemy action, including about 81,400 houses and shop flats, of which number 3,092 were either totally wrecked or subsequently had to be demolished. Serious though this might sound, the most tragic result was of course the loss of life caused by the raids, and recent research has revealed

One of the many civilian war graves in Greenbank Cemetery. This gravestone commemorates Victor Pearce, aged four, who was killed in the King Square Shelter, Carolina Row, on 2 December 1940. *(Author's Collection)*

The side of St Nicholas Church facing Baldwin Street still shows the scars made by fragments of high explosive bombs. *(Author's Collection)*

that in Bristol and adjoining Filton some 1,378 people were killed and 3,240 injured by German bombs. Numbers, however, mean little as each unfortunate person whose life was so brutally cut short represents a personal tragedy to the family and friends left behind, and the shattering effects of this can often still be felt over 70 years later.

In spite of the battering Bristol received, the Germans top priority, the destruction of the docks and their associated industries had not been accomplished, the workings of the Port of Bristol only being interrupted for one day in the four years of the bombing campaign. Likewise, although serious damage had been inflicted during attempts against the local aircraft industry, the delays in production these operations caused were made up relatively quickly and output went from strength to strength as the war progressed. Serious though the destruction and loss of life had been in Bristol, it pales into insignificance when compared with that suffered by German cities. An example being Dresden, where on the night of 13 February 1945 some 50,000 people lost their lives, the result of 805 British bombers having dropped over 1,400 tons of high explosives and about 1,200 tons of incendiaries, more than fell on Bristol during the entire war! With this in mind it becomes immediately apparent that the Luftwaffe, designed as a tactical weapon operating in close support of the army, and devoid of a successful four-engined bomber, had in fact never possessed the necessary equipment to succeed in a long drawn out strategic campaign. In the final analysis a lack of suitable equipment coupled with an inability to realise the importance of quickly following up any attack, dogged the Luftwaffe throughout the war, and when one takes into consideration Britain's ever improving air defences, we have probably identified the most important reasons for their lack of success.

During World War Two, the clamp down on civil liberties, shortages, and the effects of the bombing brought out in Bristolians a wide variety of human reactions, and although some people displayed the worst side of human nature, many performed acts of great heroism in actions far beyond the normal call of duty. With the city suffering 584 air raid alerts and bombs falling in the area on 76 occasions, the military defenders of Bristol were obviously in great danger whenever the Luftwaffe was overhead, and this can be seen by the fact that between June 1940 and May 1944 two searchlight operators, three fighter pilots, three men engaged in bomb disposal, five anti-aircraft gunners and six balloon operators made the supreme sacrifice. Back in the dark days of 1940 and 1941 the local civilian uniformed services had also been under terrific pressure, none more so than the fire fighters who lost 29 men tackling the conflagrations in Bristol, while the Warden's Service,

Sailors clearing debris in Bridge Street following the raid of 24 November. They were from HMS *Cabot*, the RN Training Establishment housed in three of the Muller's Orphan houses at Ashley Down. *(Jim Facey)*

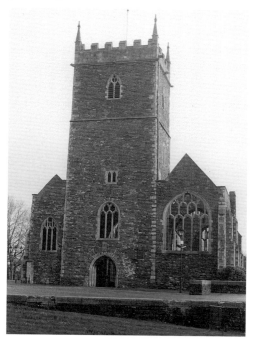

St Peter's Church in Castle Park. Burnt out during the raid of 24 November 1940, the shell has been preserved as a memorial to the suffering of Bristol during the Blitz. Two slate tablets and a series of metal plaques are attached to the base of the tower. The upper left hand tablet reads: 'In memory of the citizens of Bristol and surrounding areas who died in the blitz during the 1939–1945 war', while the right hand one tells us that it was: 'Unveiled by the Lord Mayor of Bristol to commemorate the 60th anniversary of the departure of Bristol's wartime evacuees during 1941. A special memory for the people of Bristol'.

Below these, the metal plaques record the names of the: 'Civilians and Auxiliary personnel who lost their lives during the air raids carried out between June 1940 and May 1944. They live in the memory of the living'. *(Author's Collection)*

also suffered 29 members killed in service as a result of enemy action, plus a further 134 seriously wounded. The city's Rescue Parties were also kept very busy and during the raids received 482 calls, rescued 697 people and extricated 833 bodies from demolished buildings, their courage and tenacity helping Bristol's Civil Defence Services to earn a total of four George Medals, one OBE, five MBEs, 10 BEMs and 11 Commendations for Brave Conduct in Civil Defence.

Today, little, except for a series of beautifully designed windows in Bristol Cathedral dedicated to the St John Ambulance, the Nursing Services, the British Red Cross Society, the Fire Services, Bristol Police, the Wardens Service and the Woman's Voluntary Service, remains to illustrate the sacrifice and devotion to duty shown by members of the civilian uniformed services during World War Two. Nevertheless, their untiring work on behalf of their fellow citizens must never be forgotten and their proud record should provide a fine example to Bristolians for many years to come. Likewise, the shell of St Peter's Church in Castle Park, preserved as a monument to the civilians who lost their lives in Bristol and surrounding area, and the accompanying book of remembrance on display in St Stephen's Church, are there as constant reminders of the 'blitz', while the sight of the neat and uniform rows of war graves in Greenbank Cemetery, where both British and German victims of the 'Battle of Bristol' lie peacefully together, should surely be enough evidence to future generations of the price paid by so many people to ensure their personal freedom.

INDEX

Abbots Leigh 164, 175
Adams, Rowland 88
Adler Tag 57
Air Raid Precautions Department 13
Air Raid Precautions System 26
Alderman Cox 122
All Saints' Church 86
Allied Commanders 185
Almondsbury 55, 59, 65, 127, 151
American Red Cross Club 171
Anderson, Sir John 14
Andover 40
Appleby, Matthew 60
Armed Forces Communiqué 68, 124
Army Act 162
ARP Act 13, 164
Ashley Down 171, 188
Ashton Court 171
Ashton Court Park 171
Ashton Park 120, 127, 151
Atkin, William Herbert 107–08
Avebury 118
Avon Vale Fire Fighters 121
Avonmouth 33, 35–36, 41, 46, 48–50,
   55–57, 59–60, 68, 93, 106, 117–19,
   122, 127, 134–35, 137–43, 145, 151,
   167–68, 170, 174–76, 186
Avonmouth Docks 19, 26, 40, 42, 44,
   50, 54, 117, 119–20, 135, 141, 157,
   164, 168, 171, 175–77
Avonvale Road 121
Axminster 127
Babdown Farm 55
Backwell 56, 151
Badminton Junior School 26
Baedeker Bombers 166
Baedeker Raids 167–68
Baldwin, Stanley 12
Baldwin Street 60, 82, 88, 116, 187
Balkans 135, 166
Bancroft, Mr Reginald 48
Barfleur, Point de 143
Barton Hill 77, 121
Bath 21, 28, 54, 91, 101, 107, 130, 167,
   173
Bath Buildings 107
Bath Home Guard 173
Batheaston 180
Bathurst Basin 50, 127
Beachy Head 139, 143
Beaufighter 63, 117–18, 129, 135, 138,
   140, 143, 168
Beaufighters 41
Beauforts 41
Beauvais 169
Bedminster 26, 55, 109, 111–12, 115,
   145, 150–51, 153, 156–57, 171
Bedminster Down 55
Beggars Bush Lane 175
Berkeley Square 114

Bibury 55, 59, 93
Birkenhead Docks 158
Birmingham 12, 27, 67, 70, 73, 100,
   106, 127, 135, 142, 156–57, 186
Birmingham Hospital Saturday Fund
   Home 27
Bishopsworth 12, 164
Bitton 166
Black Down 70
Blackboy Hill 127
Blackburne, Very Revd H.W. 32
Blenheim 40, 46, 118
Bofors 35, 123
Bomb Disposal Section 61
Bomb Disposal Squad 145
Bomber Command 44
Bomber Group 9
Bomber Wing 9
Bourges 123
Bournemouth 68, 78
Bradley, General 175, 184–85
Bradley, Mervyn 57
Bradley, Omar N. 175
Braund, Frank 132
Braund, Mrs 132, 134
Bray, Mrs Rhoda 22
Brean Down 168
Bremen 168
Brest Knickebein 73
Brickfields 36, 103, 141, 151
Bridewell 26
Bridge Street 21, 72, 88, 91, 102, 110,
   116, 188
Brislington 21, 46–47, 164, 167, 171
Bristol, Dean of 32
Bristol, Lord Mayor of 11, 98, 123, 188
Bristol Beaufighter 63, 118
Bristol Cathedral 189
Bristol Channel 54, 68, 117, 166
Bristol Evening Post 6–7, 21–22
Bristol Evening World 122
Bristol General Hospital 27, 101, 114
Bristol Maternity Hospital 132
Bristol Royal Infirmary 27–28
British Red Cross Society 189
Broad Weir 71, 114, 169–70
Broadfield Down 158
Broadmead 26, 115, 148
Brockley Combe 70
Brockworth 118
Brophy, John 160
Brosig, Unteroffizier Herbert 65–66
Brunswick Square 149
Bryant Street 90
Buston, Eric 81
Camberley 169
Cambrai-Epinoy 116
Cardiff 40, 50, 78, 127, 170
Castle Moat 88
Castle Park 12, 18–89

Castle Street 77, 86, 88–89, 131
Chapman, Colonel A.F. 41, 161
Chapman, Lieutenant Colonel A.F. 41
Charmy Down 39, 91, 119, 143, 172,
   181
Cheltenham Road 148
Chew Magna 70, 93, 95
Chew Magna Starfish 112, 119
Chew Stoke 151
Chippenham 48
Christian Association 10
Churchill, Brigadier 173
Churchill, Winston 41, 151, 186
City Mill 102
City Museum 163
Clergy Daughters School 184
Clevedon 117, 130
Clifford, Major 40
Clifton 26, 30, 36, 77, 83, 95, 99, 129,
   153–54, 161, 165, 175, 180, 185
Clifton College 170, 174, 184–85
Clifton Down 82, 129, 154
Clifton Parish Church 83
Closton Avenue 145
Colerne 91, 134–35, 143, 158, 168,
   178, 181
College Green 13, 86, 163
Colston Hall 163
Colston Street 149
Comer, Mr 107
Congresbury 61
Cook, Dorothy 102
Cossham Memorial Hospital 27
Cotham 83, 95, 101, 112, 129, 148
Cotham Hill 83
Coventry 67, 70, 73, 82, 100, 104, 106,
   142
Cowes 167
Crew, Flying Officer Edward 140
Cribbs Causeway 36
Cromwell Road 157
Cumberland Basin 36
Cunard 88
Cunningham, Flight Lieutenant John 138
Cunningham, Squadron Leader John 143
Cunningham, Wing Commander John
   168
Daily Express 125
Daily Telegraph 169
Dakotas 184
Dean Street 98
De Santis, Miriam 47
De Santis, Miss V. 47
Dieppe 73, 94, 135, 137, 139
Dieppe Knickebein 73
Dimbleby, Richard 163
Dinton 129
Dornier 9, 42–43, 48, 57, 59, 73, 95,
   106–08, 112, 117, 167–69, 176
Dresden 187

Dreux 73
Drew, Squadron Leader P.E. 46
Dungeness 127
Dunkirk 8, 121
Dunning, Clifford Bruce 64
Durdham Down 171
Eagle Day 57
Earthcott 150–51
Eastern House School 27
Easton 36, 114, 129–32, 164
Easton in Gordano 36, 164
Eastville 77, 129, 163
Eastville Park 163
Eden, Anthony 40
Edwards, Pilot Officers H.D. 54
Elektron 9
Ellbroad Street 131
Elles, Sir Hugh 24–25, 106, 151
Ellis, Gladys Ruth 98
Elmdale Road 83, 150
Embassy Cinema 83
Emergency Powers 20
Empire Gallantry Medal 61
English Channel 49
Essen 168
Evacuation Hospital 171
Exeter 44, 55, 91, 167
Eye Hospital 46, 149
Facey, Dave 7
Facey, Jim 6, 15, 45, 64–65, 71–72, 74,
    76–88, 91–92, 94, 96, 104–05,
    109–13, 115–16, 121, 128–31,
    133–34, 136, 139, 141–42, 144, 146,
    150–54, 156–57, 188
Fagnani, Miss M. 149
Failand 62, 64, 127, 150
Fécamp 73, 143
Filton 12, 15, 33, 35–36, 39–41, 44,
    54–58, 62, 64–68, 119, 124, 138,
    145, 161, 166, 171, 174–75, 184,
    186–87
Filton Fort 174
Filton Harriers 67
Filton Royce 66
Fire Guard Plan 172
Fokes, Sergeant R.H. 54
Fordingbridge 60
Fort Portishead 174
Frampton, Sister Violet Eva Alice 132–34
Franklin, Rosina 47
Franklin, William 47
Freiburg 7
Frenchay 28, 171, 184–85
Frenchay Hospital 171, 184–85
Frenchay Park 28
Galitzine, Emanuel 170
Gem Cinema 102
German Ministry of Propaganda 179
German News Agency 178, 180, 182
Geschwader 9, 67, 179
Geschwader Group 9
Gibbs, George 26
Gibson, Lieutenant Colonel N.G. 161
Gillard, Frank 163

Gillingham 54
Glascoed 68
Glasgow 50, 67, 127, 141, 184
Glenarm Walk 46–47
Gloster 39, 118
Gloucester 34, 35, 39, 106
Gloucestershire Home Guard 161
Gloucestershire Regiment 34
Göring, Reichsmarschall Hermann 61
Gomm, Stephen 21
Good Friday Raid 142, 149, 152
Goodwin, Hubert 47–48
Gordon Road 22
Gourock 184
Götz, Unteroffizier Horst 169
Great George Street 184
Greenbank Cemetery 29, 31, 65–66,
    123–24, 186, 189
Grunert, George 175
Guthrie, Sergeant Norman 140
Haig, Field Marshal 185
Hambrook 55, 127
Hamburg 176, 178
Handley Page 102
Handley, Tommy 163
Hanham 12, 55, 151
Hares, Bill 99, 102, 114, 130, 148
Harford Street 46
Harms, Oberleutnant Otto-Bernard 95
Harris, Eliza 47
Haslar 157, 167
Hastings 179
Hawker Hurricane 13, 36, 39
Haydon 65
Headley Park 182
Heinkel 9, 42–44, 46, 48, 51, 54,
    56–57, 59–60, 62, 64, 67–68, 73, 76,
    101, 106, 108, 118–19, 122–24, 129,
    135, 137, 139–41, 143, 156, 166–67,
    176–77
Henbury 55, 65, 127
Hendon 7, 65
Henfield 150–51
Henleaze 175
Hewish 140
High Cross 86
High Street 71–72, 77–79, 83–84, 110,
    113, 115–16
Hill Deverill 180
Hodge, Valerie 18
Hollinde, Oberleutnant 124
Home Guard 41, 120–22, 160–62,
    164–65, 172–74, 183, 186
Home Office 13, 17–19, 22
Hooper, Mr F.C. 7
Horfield 26, 142, 145
Hosie, Unteroffizier Wolfgang 158
Hotwells 90, 112
Höhenkampfkommando 168
Hull 46, 127, 134
Hullavington 48, 55
Hyde Park 18
Identity Cards 20
Imperial War Museum 7

Irish Sea 68
James, Ian 7
Jones, George 108
Jones, Sergeant H.D.B. 65
Joyce, William 104
Junkers 9, 42–43, 48, 51, 54, 57–60,
    67–68, 70, 95, 101, 106, 108, 112,
    118–19, 129–30, 134–35, 137, 139,
    143, 158, 166–70, 176–77, 182
Kenn Moor 70
Kewstoke 27
Keynsham 59, 82, 151, 166
King George VI 18, 125
King, Mr E.W. 63
Kings Weston 182
Kingsdown 129, 131–33, 148
Kingston Seymour 70
Kingswood 12, 27, 146
Kless, Major Friedrich 63
Lambeth 7
Langer, Hauptmann Siegfried 168
Lawrence Hill 106, 130–32
Lawrence Weston 55, 59
Le Havre 137, 139
Lee, General John C.H. 185
Leeds 12
Lennard's 83–84
Lewis Guns 35, 122, 173
Lighting Restrictions Order 21
Liverpool 12, 50, 59–60, 67, 94, 100,
    127, 141, 153, 186
Local Defence Volunteers 10, 40
Lodge Farm 142, 151
Lohmann, Oberleutnant Hermann 123
London 8, 12, 56, 60–62, 67, 69–70, 76,
    78, 94, 104, 106, 118, 122, 127,
    134–35, 149, 170, 177–78, 186
Long Ashton 55, 121, 174
Lord Beaverbrook 125
Lord Haw Haw 104
Lord Woolton 159
Louis, Joe 184
Lower Maudlin Street 45–46
Lulsgate Bottom 158
Lutz, Hauptmann Martin 66
Lübeck 166
Lydlinch 143
Lyme Bay 40, 135, 137, 143
Lyme Regis 139
Lympshan 158
Lyndon Hotel 170
Manchester 12, 118
Mangotsfield 12
Mardon 90
Markham 151
Maunder, Superintendent Albert 135
Mauritania 86
McGrath, Mr 107
Meacons 156–57
Meek, Frederick 46, 47
Merchant Street 99, 102
Merville 46
Messerschmitt 9, 10, 42, 48, 61–62,
    65–67, 167, 176

Middle Wallop 40, 46, 55, 135
Milbrook Avenue 21
Montpelier 106–07, 129
Morley, George 7
Morrison, Herbert 14
Munich 8, 13
Nailsea 167
Narrow Wine Street 81, 88
Newent 106
Newfoundland Street 99
Newport 50, 78
Noel, Miss Rosina 47–48
Noel, Mrs 47–48
Nokes-Cooper, Pilot Officer B. 46
Normandy 8, 184–85
North Street 82, 99, 151
Northolt 170
Northover 173–74
Norwich 167
Oldbury Naite 166
Olveston 59
Operation Ibex 10
Operation Layers 10, 103, 112, 118–19
Operation Layers Original 10
Operation Sealion 10, 56
Ostend 143
Park Row 85, 149, 161
Park Street 76, 85–86, 89, 149, 184
Parnall 35–36, 41–42, 56, 65, 68, 118,
   122–25
Pembrey 44, 54
Perseus 41
Philadelphia Street 131, 170
Pilning 142, 151
Plymouth 73, 78, 94, 100, 118, 134,
   181, 186
Poole Bay 137
Portbury 55, 122–24, 151
Portbury Wharf 122–24
Portishead 33, 35–36, 41, 46, 48, 50–51,
   60, 62, 123, 142–43, 151, 174
Portishead Docks 48, 50–51, 142
Portland 62, 111, 143
Portsmouth 73, 118, 127, 181
Portview Road 157
Portway 157
Pucklechurch 34, 36
Purdown 36–38, 95, 103, 141, 151, 164
Queen Charlotte Street 88
Rawnsley, Flight Lieutenant C.F. Jimmy
   168
Rawnsley, Sergeant C.F. Jimmy 138, 143
Reading, Marchioness of 17
Redcliff 89, 102
Redcliff Hill 90, 175
Redcliff Street 116, 149
Redfield 95
Redland 98, 106, 129, 138
Redland Green 138
Regent Cinema 86, 88
Reiser, Feldwebel Martin 73
Rennes 143
Reynolds, Lieutenant Edward Womersley
   61

Ritterkruz 63
River Avon 26, 110–11, 120, 172
River Frome 80
River Seine 42
Robins, Annie Caroline 114
Rockingham 36, 151
Rodway 134, 151
Rose, Frederick 58
Rosemary Street 100, 149
Rostock 167
Royal Edward Dock 93, 119, 176
Royal West of England Sanatorium 27
Royce, Flying Officer Michael 65
Rudloe Manor 54
St Andrew Road 157
St Anselm's Church 82
St James's Barton 78, 84, 92
St John Ambulance 189
St Joseph's Home 83
St Martin's Hospital 28
St Michael's Hill 98–99, 133, 138, 149
St Monica's Home 28
St Nicholas Church 83, 88, 91, 187
St Peter's Church 12, 64, 188–89
St Philip's Marsh 101
St Philips 77, 106, 108
St Stephen's Church 189
Salisbury 94, 166, 170
Saunders, C.H. 54
Saunders, George 47
Scampton 102
Sealion 10, 56
Selsey Bill 143
Severn Beach 55
Severn Estuary 54, 57, 68, 112, 117,
   122, 166
Severn Tunnel 168
Shaftesbury 46, 101, 168, 181
Sheffield 12, 127
Shirehampton 26, 41, 93, 106, 122, 141,
   171
Shirehampton Park 141, 171
Simpson, General William H. 184
Smith, Canon J.S. 148
Smith, Mr Henry George 22
Sommer, Leutnant Erich 169
Southampton 44, 46, 56, 70, 94, 100,
   104, 106, 111, 122, 169, 184
Southmead 27
Southville 90
Speck von Sternburg, Oberleutnant
   Johannes 68
Spitfire 16, 36, 41, 49, 59, 170
Stanford, Herbert 90
Stanley Close 22
Stanstead 169
Stapleton Road 127, 129
Stevens, Assistant Matron Elsie Lilian
   132–34
Stinchcombe, Florence 47
Stockwood 70, 95, 103, 112, 166
Stockwood Starfish 166
Stoke Bishop 175
Stoke Gifford 64

Stokes Croft 82, 99, 131, 148, 149
Swansea 44, 50, 122
Talbot-Plumb, Captain 40
Temple Church 87
Temple Combe 182
Temple Meads 94, 99, 101–02, 112, 182
Temple Street 61, 87, 89
Tetbury 55
Thames Estuary 117
Thomas, Wynford-Vaughan 163
Tiepelt, Oberleutnant Hans 65
Trinity Church 81
Trym 26, 139, 164, 175
Tyndall 25
Underdown, Alderman T.H.J. 11, 123,
   126
Union Street 74, 80, 88
University Road 84
Vannes 57, 93, 111
Vickers 34–35, 173
Victoria Rooms 83
Victoria Street 20, 85, 89–90
Villacoublay 73
Wadman, Mrs Caroline 107–08
Wakefield, Ken 7
Warmley 130
Warmwell 62
Watts, Jack 47
Webb, Herbert 26
Wells Road 30, 145
Western Daily Press 47, 81
Westland 62, 66
Weston 55, 59, 117, 182
Weymouth 183
Whatley, Ellen 47
Whitchurch 12, 55, 65, 104, 141, 151,
   172, 174
Whitchurch Fort 174
White, Sir Stanley 40
Whitehall 22, 129
Whiteladies Cinema 83
Whiteladies Road 81–82, 95–96
Wide, Horace 47
Williams, Flight Lieutenant E.S. 39
Willway Street 156, 157
Windgap 170
Winford 28, 179
Winford Orthopaedic Hospital 28
Winterbourne 36
Wintle, Charles 47
Woodland Road 25, 85
World War One 16, 34–35, 41
World War Two 7, 8, 30, 62, 65, 110,
   119, 123–24, 169, 182–83, 187, 189
Worrall Road 36
Wraxall House 174
Wright, Flight Lieutenant A.R. 59
Yatton 68
Yeomouth 70
Yeovil 62, 66, 179
Yeovilton 183
York 167, 172, 175
YWCA Hostel 114

L'Armee D'Henri V: Bourgeois-Gentilshommes Arriere-Ban De L'Ordre Moral, 1873-1874

Adolphe Bouillet